EXORCIST RISING

A Magico-Religious Primer

NOAH TYSICK

Copyright © 2012 Noah Tysick
All rights reserved.

A New Voodoo City™ Publication
www.newvoodoocity.com

ISBN 13: 978-0615615387
ISBN 10: 0615615384

For Ryan

I am not afraid—I was born to do this.

~St. Joan of Arc

CONTENTS

1	This Present Darkness	1
2	The Ethics of Evil	7
3	Demonology Reconsidered	15
4	Serpent Speak	30
5	The Newer Rite	38
6	Traditional Prayers	95
7	Magico-Religious Psalms	115
	Bibliography	

EXORCIST RISING

1 THIS PRESENT DARKNESS

A "scream" is always just that – a noise and not music.

~Carl Jung

The "Liberation"
I stopped believing in a literal devil about a decade ago. Graduate school and so-called common sense led me to the conclusion that the Satan of my childhood was an artifact of the human experience—a way to explain atrocities and the seemingly random. By assigning a name to tragedy and misfortune, I could blame the exact cause of all my ills on "The Devil."

It was morally and psychologically convenient—a mechanism of self-preservation in times of extreme horror or devastation. Without a proverbial witch to burn, misfortune begged the invention of Satan, Beelzebub, Lucifer, and myriad nameless demons. Like any other reasonable, educated individual, I no longer had the need to assign blame. Personal accountability replaced the necessity for a mythological scapegoat, and simple cause-and-effect was more plausible than outdated superstition. Although I never denied a Higher Force or God, evil proper became much more relative to the point of being nonexistent.

I was liberated by my newfound pragmatism, and all the planets of my personal cosmos fell into line quite nicely. The shackles of religion fell impotent at my self-satisfied feet. Like *Rosemary's Baby* and *The Exorcist*, Satan was nothing more than a cinematic flicker in my childhood mind. The adult in me experienced the harsh realities of life without needing to "plead the blood of Jesus" or "drive out any devils."

If we're honest with ourselves, we tend to live on autopilot most of the time. We go to work or school, pay our bills, take care of what our version of family is, and we try to enjoy some downtime. While it's rare that people strictly adhere to the faith of their upbringing, it is true that most have no need to reconsider the religious, social, moral, and political ideals learned in childhood.

Our actions are the result of "reflexive thinking"—that is, we are content with our inherited biases and have no need to consider other perspectives or worldviews.[1] Simply stated, it's much easier to accept the way things have always been. To challenge what comes automatic is to invite emotional crisis and existential angst.

Dr. Jack Mezirow, Learning Theorist and Professor Emeritus at Columbia, calls this type of crisis a "disorienting dilemma," which he proposes is a perquisite for authentic ("transformative") learning.[2] When faced with this type of predicament, we have the opportunity to engage in a critical reconsideration of our current intellectual, religious, and social filters. Our conclusions may include some of what we

---

[1] Gergen, M. M. & Gergen, K. J. (2003). Qualitative inquiry: Tensions and transformations. In N. K. Denzin & Y. S. Lincoln (Eds.) *The Landscape of qualitative research: Theories and issues*. (p. 579). Thousand Oaks: Sage Publications.

[2] Mezirow, J. (2000). *Learning as Transformation: Critical Perspectives on a Theory in Progress*. (pp. 9-11 & 17-18) San Francisco: Jossey Bass.

were originally taught, but it will be based on our own findings rather than a mindless continuation of tradition.[3]

The Invitation

It was January, and the City of Brotherly Love had the color of a black light with pinholes of white shining from the underside. From my fourteenth floor hotel room, I could see some sort of clock tower and an invisible grid of power lines pulsing with red at their tallest points—some sort of warning for low-flying aircraft. The sounds outside were completely blocked behind the thick glass that refused to frost even in the coldest conditions. My agenda? To see the Liberty Bell, visit the home of Edgar Allen Poe, and to receive a "head washing" at the first Humofor (Haitian Voodoo Temple) to receive a 501(c)(3) status in the United States. According to the IRS, it was a legitimate organization—the real deal.

Their website showed the basics, but I wanted to be on the inside. I wanted to be initiated into one of the most mysterious and taboo belief systems in existence. I had experienced the Divine in New Orleans—both in Catholic and Voodoo-esque contexts, in the Buddhist temples of Chicago, the Holiness Pentecostal (snake handling) churches of rural Michigan, in the presence of His Holiness the 14th Dalai Lama, and in Spiritualist Camps like those of Lilydale, New York. In every religious or spiritual context to date, I saw the Divine. My confidence in the innate goodness and redeeming quality of every sincere seeker was unshaken. Every place of worship or shrine I ever visited demonstrated the complexity of God and the false limitations I had placed on him/her. I was always taught that Jesus was the only way, but I knew he didn't play favorites. I just had to see for myself.

After several days of texting and telephone interviews with different elders of the Voodoo Peristyle in Philadelphia, I was given an official invitation to attend a ceremony with

---

[3] Ibid.

the possibility of initiation. I was told the time and exact location of the next days' event would be made known a couple hours before it would happen. The secrecy was as suspicious as it was intoxicating, and I felt privileged to be granted entrance by the Gro Mambo herself.

The Visitation

The windows were covered, and the only light in the room was the glow of the large television with the sound turned down to an almost imperceptible level. I was asked politely to remove my shoes, and someone took my coat. We were not at the main temple in the city; rather, we were at the home of Gro Mambo herself. She remained in the upper part of the townhouse while I sat in an overstuffed leather chair speaking with three senior members. There was constant action, which made it difficult for me to focus on the conversation at hand. A steady flow of people and their children walked silently through the living room into the kitchen? Basement? I couldn't see beyond the shallow field of light or the hinged room divider just across from me. I heard the faint sounds of food being prepared and what sounded like the shuffle of significant sums of cash—lots of counting.

After nearly two hours of sitting in the darkness with an increasingly intense, almost interrogative conversation with one gentleman in particular (assigned to me?), I began to feel fatigued and drowsy. The percussive sound of drumming began in the basement below; their hypnotic rhythm could be felt in the soles of my feet.

I felt panic begin to well up within me as my mentor said not to worry about time. "The Loa will decide when we begin and when they're finished."

He continued, "We told the cab driver that just arrived that you didn't need a ride back to your hotel. Did you say you had to meet someone, or did you come to the city on your own?"

I tried to hide any semblance of anxiety, "Friends are expecting me. I can only stay for a few hours."

"I'll personally see that you get to where you need to go, Mr. Noah;" he wasn't allowing me the option to decline.

My hotel was nearly 20 miles away, and I was in a residential area outside of the city that likely didn't have taxis on demand. The drumming below was gaining momentum, and I was at the mercy of my host. Without a cab, I had no out. Without my coat, I had no phone. As I began to feel the increasing urgency of my situation, the man's countenance suddenly shifted.

His face became angular, and I thought my eyes were playing tricks on me. The steady flow of people stopped, and it was just the two of us left in the front room. He went from looking at me through two eyes into gazing through only one—the other sunk into submission. I was no longer in the presence of a man. The Thing behind the animated eye spoke slowly, deliberately. Its breathing was labored; its gazed fixed.

"What... do... **you**... *really*... want?"

At this moment, my disbelief in The Devil was irrelevant. I went from postulating to knowing.

NOAH TYSICK

2 THE ETHICS OF EVIL

Disease, insanity, and death were the angels that attended my cradle, and since then have followed me throughout my life.

~Edvard Munch

We Can't Begin Like This

I've written this book with a bit of trepidation. There will be cynics that will have already made up their minds before cracking the cover. While some will read every page, they'll quickly dismiss my claims based on two primary factors: I operate independently of any ecclesiastical approval—particularly that of the Roman Catholic Church, and I lack that one salacious tale upon which to hang my self-satisfied hat. In other words, I have no Lutz family[4] or Robbie Mannheim[5] listed on my resume.

While I may use some Catholic elements in my practice, I do not presume they are the sole authority in matters of

---

[4] The couple allegedly tormented by an evil presence in their Amityville home on Oceanside Drive

[5] The "real-life demoniac" used as the basis for William Peter Blatty's *The Exorcist*

Spirit. This includes the "authorized" Roman Ritual (of Exorcism). As for infamous cases of demonic infestations of homes and individuals, I approach these with a healthy amount of skepticism. I wasn't at the Amityville home at 112 Ocean Avenue, and I was not alive during the exorcism(s) of the little boy upon which *The Exorcist* is based. I can't speak to either of these specific cases.

Everything I present in this short volume should also be approached with skepticism. Although I consider myself a man of integrity, I encourage you to question any claims I make, but I also ask you to do so with a receptive mind. At minimum, you'll have a greater awareness of another perspective of demonology and the ever-controversial issue of exorcism. Ideally, you'll have some tools to help you navigate any potential demonic encounters that present themselves. Additionally, I hope this will give you a starting point for your own paranormal research or magico-religious practice. Like terrorists or viruses, demons are not one-trick ponies—their methods are far from static. They acclimate to their environment and modify their approach to avoid extinction. Our best defense is to remain vigilant and adaptable.

The Problem of Evil
With the belief in a God or Higher Power comes an automatic acceptance of evil. We can only know something as "good" by its relationship to something else—otherwise, everything would just *be*. Relativity is the only way to explain the nature of a thing. In other words, we classify the things in our world by comparing them to others.

The Western idea of The Problem of Evil isn't anything new. More disturbing, it's something we'll never completely reconcile or understand. Philosophers, theologians, and millennia of seeking come back to the same fundamental questions. The basic premise is this: The Universe was created by an all-knowing, all good, and all-powerful being we call God; however, evil exists. This presents the following:

> If this God truly knows all, (s)he would have had the foresight to prevent the opportunity for evil from the outset.
>
> If (s)he is all good, God wouldn't be able to conceive of creating anything inherently evil or capable of evil.
>
> If (s)he is all-powerful, there would be no evil. If it tried to manifest in some way, God wouldn't allow it.

So where does this leave us? The origin and acceptance of what we consider "evil" leave us scratching our heads at best. It's predicated on the belief that there is a God, and something went wrong.

This original Problem of Evil is further complicated when we take other factors into consideration. What if you don't believe in God? What about other religions? Is evil a sort of discarnate energy, or is it something intelligent and fixed? How do we separate the "good" from the "bad"? In other words, malevolent behavior or beings require a universal definition of evil.

I'm going to propose a very simple question. I ask that you don't hesitate or overthink it. Just give a kneejerk "yes" or "no." Ready? Here it is (again, just go with your first instinct):

Is fire a good thing or a bad thing?

Without further consideration, choose if it should be placed in the good or bad column of your own checklist of morality. Holding onto that first impression, please think about these scenarios.

> It's late autumn, and you're lost in the woods. Night and the reality of being in the middle of nowhere is creeping up quickly. You have matches but no tent, shelter, or flashlight.
>
> You've spent a couple hundred dollars on fireworks, and it's the evening of the Fourth of July.
>
> You just finished building your dream home complete with electric furnace and central air.
>
> You're a burn victim.

Considering the context and circumstances, it isn't possible to definitively say that fire is a gift or a curse. We can't simply declare something is evil without making granular distinctions. Before looking at the demonic, it's essential to establish whether or not something is evil, which leads us back to our main question: How do we determine if something is inherently evil?

> ✶ Consider this...
> "Angel" or "angels" appear in the King James Version of the Bible 283 times, "devil" or "devils" are mentioned 106 times and "demon" or "demons" do not appear at all.

Cultural Considerations

Hindu devotees of Lord Krishna believe cows to be sacred. Nandi the Divine Bull is a powerful vehicle (sort of like a sidekick or familiar) for Krishna and his wife Radha. Cows are a gift of God rather than a source of protein and iron, but drinking their milk is like a sacrament. Conversely, eating the flesh of a cow is sacrilege and would result in bad karma.

Christians have no particular rules regarding cows. Unless one chooses to be a vegetarian for health or other reasons not based on religion, steak and hamburger are perfectly acceptable sources of nourishment. Christians consider the Bible to be holy—it's the most sacred text in existence. For this reason, the pages are often leafed in gold and bound in a durable, **leather** cover.

The tendency is to throw up our hands and say that the determination of what is or isn't evil is up to individuals to decide—it depends on your culture and personal beliefs. This is a dangerous approach (and the main reason for such division within American culture and throughout the Middle East). Even if only conceptually, the cross-cultural consensus is that evil exists in some form. The challenge is in consistently determining what is innately evil.

Christians and Hindus agree that consumption of dairy products is morally acceptable. Hinduism reveres the cow as God dwelling among humanity in the form of Nandi. Christian scripture is the Word of God that is usually bound in the tanned skin of this sacred animal. Are Krishna devotees[6] wrong even though their religion predates Christianity by about 2,000 years? Are bible publishing houses evil? Western philosophy would argue these aren't valid questions; that is, we're asking the wrong thing.

Philosophical Considerations & Common Sense

Generally speaking, philosophy is divided into four main categories: Ethics, Metaphysics, Epistemology, and Aesthetics. The first two are of particular relevance when considering the thousand pound question (i.e. How can we know if something is truly evil?)

---

[6] Not to be confused with the Hare Krishna Movement/Cult started in the New York in the mid 1960s. Hinduism practitioners worship God by different names and devote themselves to that "version" of the Divine.

In the example of the sacred cow, evil doesn't seem relevant. A reasonable person wouldn't label Hinduism as fundamentally wicked, nor would he or she say with certainty that manufacturing bibles is evil. The real consideration is one of ethics.

Ethics is the branch of philosophy that explores and defines morals and acceptable behaviors within a given culture. While some may base life choices on religious teachings, one does not need to practice religion to be moral. Aristotle contends that being "good" is defined in the way the majority of a society conducts themselves. Furthermore, the "good of the many" is composed of two factors, which are "virtue of mind" and "virtue of character."[7] The process by which we determine "goodness" and morality is a cultural construct founded on our ability to consciously use what we have been taught to do and to demonstrate this through consistently adhering to an agreed upon set of rules. Doing the right thing is an ongoing intellectual process whereby we gain the respect of our peers. Being known as a person of integrity is its own reward, which is entirely separate from religion and the dichotomy of "holy vs. evil." Perhaps our crisis is rooted in our common misunderstanding of the distinction between Ethics and Metaphysics, which is the other branch of philosophy that's relevant in this case—Metaphysics is the territory in which we hammer out the questions of God, The Devil, the nature of evil, and all things spiritual and supernatural.

While philosophy is the starting point of all human inquiry, it isn't the destination. An idea may begin within the sphere of the philosophical, but it typically transfers into another area of study or practice. More specifically, questions regarding celestial bodies began in the realm of Metaphysics. As answers started to emerge (i.e. the earth is not the center of the universe), they were translated into the hard sciences of Astronomy and Physics. Divinity and the supernatural

---

[7] Kraut, R. (2010). Aristotle's Ethics. *Stanford encyclopedia of philosophy online.* Retrieved from http://plato.stanford.edu/entries/aristotle-ethics/

remain under the philosophical umbrella of Metaphysics, but they also hold a place outside of the sciences (e.g. the paranormal, the supernatural, parapsychology, and the like).

The evil or demonic is too complex for a singular methodology of inquiry given its ability to manifest in subtle and conspicuous ways. The ethos of a realistic approach to evil rests not in ancient writings or the supposed authority of a "qualified" exorcist; rather, it is a combination of experience, study, and continuous examination. Ultimately, the experiential takes precedence over blind faith, religious obedience, and reliance on secondhand testimony.

I said all of that to say this: We cannot *believe* or *debate* our way into understanding evil or the demonic. We have to see for ourselves.

3 DEMONOLOGY RECONSIDERED

And [Jesus] asked him, What is thy name? And he answered, saying, My name is Legion: for we are many.

~Mark 5:9 (KJV)

Demonology Among World Religions

The way we define a diabolic presence, demonic cleaving, or preternatural infestation has everything to do with the way it is expelled. This is determined by several factors that include a combination of cultural, regional, religious, educational, and socio-economic influences. This makes it difficult to establish a definitive set of criteria for detecting the absence or presence of a demon. Because of this, no single, formulaic method exists—there is no silver bullet.

Jewish Mysticism (i.e. the oral tradition of what is known as Kabbalah), tells us the Universe is not separate from God. In fact, all that we know of the physical world exists within a niche of God's Cosmic Body. Within this body are 12 Sefirot, which function as various "face" attributes of the Divine. This matrix of attributes contains both dark and light, but it all remains (very literally) within God. Of the twelve Sefirot, the one called Din is where the harshest and darkest aspect of the divine lives and emanates. More to the point, Din is the part of God that houses what we consider demons. The premise is that the demonic is a hardwired part of the cosmos, which cannot be truly driven out.

The mystical teachings of the ancient Hebrews and their sacred text known as the Zohar are not in complete alignment with more orthodox teachings as found in the Torah and, ultimately, the Christian Bible. All these teachings are predated by the Sanatana Dharma (commonly called "Hinduism") and its brother Buddhism.

Generally speaking, Hindus do not believe in a Satan figure, per se. As with the Cabbalists, all things come from "The Source." God has fierce and wrathful aspects that are

necessary to bring balance to the Universe. They aren't "good" or "bad," they are all manifestations of the same source. For instance, the Divine Mother may be loving and gentle when she manifests as Parvati, yet she becomes wild, fierce, and terrifying in the form of Kali. Many Westerners have a difficult time with this concept, but Kali is actually a "slayer of demons." Her frightening demeanor is that of a mother defending her children, and she becomes enraged when anyone or anything threatens the well-being of her offspring. It is critical to note: The "demons" Kali slays are not literal entities. They are ignorance (i.e. of our innate goodness) and representative of negative thought patterns and dangerous mindsets.

Of the several schools of Buddhism, Tibetan Buddhism lends itself most to demonology. Some even call it the

Catholicism of the Buddhist world with their focus on ritual, talismans, a centralized leader (i.e. their papal equivalent is the Dalai Lama), and opulent statuary. In addition to the historic Buddha, there is strong devotion to myriad deities. Without engaging in an exhaustive discussion of the differences between Buddhist and Western notions of theism, it is important to note a few glaring distinctions:

> **A Personal God**
> "God" is an intelligent force or "the ground of being" rather than a personal entity.
>
> **A Literal God**
> Any deities that appear in sacred texts and imagery are not thought of as literal. While there was a historic Buddha, the Buddha or "Buddha mind" is actually an ideal to which seekers aspire.
>
> **Worship and Prayer**
> The Buddha and other beings are not venerated like Christ. They are representative of various attributes or mindsets to achieve or avoid. For example, one invokes the name of Mahakala ("Lord of the Tent") for protection from fear, anger, and other destructive thought patterns. The supplicant is not calling for Divine intervention; rather, they are summoning the part of their psyche that possesses the qualities of this protector deity.

When a religion creates a "good" form of something, its antithesis is implied. To know something is positive, a negative is required. Tibetan Buddhism speaks of dakinis or "sky dancers" not unlike the Christian/Jewish/Muslim idea of angels, but the closest approximation of "evil" is "ignorance." This ignorance is in opposition to our true nature—our Buddha mind, which knows that all attachment leads to suffering. This is illustrated in the Pali canon of Buddhist writings that speak of internal struggle between our intrinsic goodness and the ideas that no longer serve us. For (Tibetan) Buddhists, Mara ("The Tempter") is the closest opposite of the dakinis and other positive celestial beings. Mara *represents* any habitual or learned behaviors that are comfortable but destructive.

Briefly stated, Tibetans make a distinction between dark and light, but it is much more conceptual than our Western equivalents. There is no external, cosmic battle between Satan and St. Michael the Archangel. Good and evil are constructs of humanity, and it is up to individuals to move from confusion to clarity—from bondage to liberation.

In the mainstream Euro-American mind, there is a definitive line between evil and good. Whether an individual subscribes to Wiccan, Pagan, or other earth-based beliefs or one of the Abrahamic traditions (Christianity, Judaism, Islam), there is a certain level of agreement that evil has form and intelligence. It occupies space and has a certain level of influence on people, places, and events. The way each of these traditions approaches the issue is in entirely different matter. This is also true when speaking from a (Judeo-Christian) magico-religious perspective. While it has the most in common with Judeo-Christian ideas, these mainstream religions would likely frown on these methodologies used to confront and expel the demonic.

What is a Demon?
We can't really know where and when demons came into existence. We are limited to religious and occult texts to provide various accounts; however, these are often symbolic and culturally biased. Unfortunately, there is no definitive text available, and any attempt to fine one is as ineffectual, complicated, and impassioned as the creationism versus evolution debate. Briefly stated, we can't truly know the causation of demons. What we *do* know is that they exist,

and the better question is: What does their title tell us about their nature?

For the last few centuries, the words "demon" and "devil" have been used interchangeably and without regard for any type of hierarchy. These are blanket terms for malevolent, destructive entities falling somewhere under the rule of a leading figure known by such names as Lucifer, Satan, Beelzebub, "Son of the Morning," The Devil (with a capital 'd'), etc. For our purposes, we can begin to understand "the nature of The Beast" with a closer examination of the word itself. The etymology (i.e. the roots and evolution of the word "demon") lends itself to a great amount of ambiguity and the potential for misinterpretation. Most arguably, Judeo-Christian application of the Latin *daemon* ("spirit") and the Greek *daimon* ("deity, divine power, lesser god, guiding spirit") implies that non-Abrahamic gods and demigods are demons. Ancient Greek and Roman gods were—quite literally—demonized.[8] Aside from this and without dwelling on our preconceived ideas of demons, the Latin and Greek roots of these beings are both vague and non-threatening at first glance.

The negative connotation of the word is the result of several complex factors. Language doesn't evolve in an orderly or linear fashion. The English Language is not a direct descendant of Latin or Greek; rather, it's the result of several tribes of people that migrated from the cradle of civilization into what is now Europe. Known as the Indo-

---

[8] Harper, D. (2011-2012). Demon. *Online etymology dictionary*. Retrieved from http://www.etymonline.com/index.php?term=demon

European family of languages, the earliest form of *dai-mon* included the base *da* or "divider" into account (i.e. "splitting, sorting, or forcing apart"), which assigned a specific attribute to the Latin and Greek versions of the word.[9] From this we can glean a more concise explanation of how our word "demon" takes on a much more sinister meaning than that of the general Greek and Latin variations. The implication is that a demon is a spirit known for its destructive nature and intention of disassembling something that is intact.

A Magico-Religious Definition of "Demon"

Based on the etymology and evolution of the term, a demon could be classified as an agent of merciless annihilation. The inference is that these types of entities subsist on the process *of* or desire *to* take that which is whole and systematically disrupting, confounding, dismembering, and mutilating it. Their motivation can't be entirely understood, but the fallout of their influence is undeniable. This is entirely consistent with the words of Jesus as shown in chapter 10 of the Gospel of John when he states, "The thief [Devil and his underlings] cometh not, but for to steal, and to kill, and to destroy [...]" (v. 10).

With an understanding of the word "demon" and a biblical description of their function, it is clear that the truly demonic involves a merciless execution of brute force. Demons have specific intentions—they exist with a purpose. They are intelligent, stealthy, relentless beings that are not to be taken lightly. It doesn't take a theologian to see the very tangible results of the darker side of spirituality. We live in a world where people do the unspeakable on a daily basis. What causes a woman to calmly and methodically drown her own children in a bathtub and pile their bodies like cordwood? Why do seemingly rational people suddenly do the unthinkable? There is cruelty, violence, unrestrained rage, blatant neglect and abuse of children, and there are large-

---

[9] Ibid.

scale attacks like genocide and ethnic cleansing. This is the bad news.

The good news is that most demonic activity is relatively subtle. The dramatic and most obvious are the exception—they are the (frequently sensationalized) minority. Blatant possession is extremely rare, but that is only one way demons impact our world. Obsession, oppression, and attachment are the most common. These will be discussed a bit later.

The *Real* Problem of Evil

Do you know any women born in the early-to-mid 1960s named Jackie or Jacqueline? How about anyone born between 1994 and 2004 named Chandler? This is no coincidence. In the 1960s, Jacqueline and Jackie ranked among the top 200 girls' names in the U.S. (ranking at 51 and 148 respectively).[10] Whether directly or subconsciously, we are influenced by popular culture. Naming a child is significant—it can define their personality and the way they are treated or perceived by others for their entire lives. This important decision isn't something folks take lightly. During the Kennedy Family's time in the White House, the masses were smitten with a new image of beauty and grace in the person of The First Lady. *Friends* was an iconic sitcom featuring Matthew Perry as a handsome, successful "nice guy." Who wouldn't want their child to emulate these qualities?

The same can be applied to just about anything that is wildly popular at any given point in our history—this includes the demonic. The formal (Catholic) Rite of Exorcism was considered a relic of the Middle Ages until William Peter Blatty's *The Exorcist* brought the satanic into our collective awareness (i.e. the book and subsequent 1970s film). The Devil has sustained and gained momentum into

---

[10] SSA. (2011). Popular baby names: Top names of the 1960s. *United States Social Security Administration Website*. Retrieved from http://www.ssa.gov/OACT/babynames/decades/names1960s.html

the new millennium by way of a steady diet of films, books, and other media outlets (e.g. *The Order, The Exorcism of Emily Rose, The Rite,* et al.), which leads to two problems: 1. An alarming number of people thinking they are possessed, and 2. An even more disturbing opportunity for emerging "exorcists." As an intelligent society, we have knowledge and resources that weren't available to past civilizations. We can successfully treat medical and psychiatric conditions that were formerly classified as demonic. Reasonable folks understand personal accountability and free will rather than dismissing behaviors as something "the devil made me do." While evil does exist, spiritual discernment and common sense should always prevail.

Exorcism Defined

> Exorcism is the process of expelling, binding, subjugating, or driving out a demon or other satanic entity through the use of prayers, incantations, chants, psalms, sacramentals, sacred oils/waters, and/or other situationally appropriate materials. Any type of spiritual cleansing or exorcism must **never** be performed in a face-to-face setting wherein a person is restrained, demeaned, provoked, locked, detained, abused, confronted, threatened, or intimidated either directly or indirectly. Exorcism is a spiritual, magico-religious process. **Aside from chirothesy, at no time should it involve touching or any type of physical contact.**

Everyone has their own presuppositions of how an exorcism is supposed to *look*. This typically includes a demoniac sitting in a chair or lying down while a priest looms over the possessed in a white cassock and purple stole. The father and his acolyte calmly recite the requisite prayers as the demon begins to contort within the host while growling blasphemies and profanities. Often the possessed is restrained "for their own good." The same ritual is repeated—over hours, days, or even months—until the entity finally leaves person.

While I can appreciate the dramatics and gothic intimations of this type of good versus evil showdown, it bears no resemblance to the type of exorcisms I perform or endorse. In addition to the almost silly display of showmanship, this approach is dangerous both physically and psychologically. Many historic cases of "traditional" exorcisms like this have resulted in death—in murder. People have been starved and restrained to the point of suffocating by those professing/attempting to help them (e.g. Anneliese Michel, real-life "Emily" of the film *The Exorcism of Emily Rose*).

> ✠ Consider this...
>
> In 2005, Maricica Cornici underwent an exorcism by her fellow nuns and parish priest. She was chained to a cross, gagged with a towel, and deprived of food and water. Three days into the "ritual," she died.

The Newer Rite of Exorcism
A magico-religious approach consists of praying *for* the afflicted—not *at* them. It is a spiritual process that takes place in the subtle or unseen realms. It is **never** a confrontation between exorcist and demon or exorcist and human. The former smacks of arrogance—the latter, of ignorance.

The contents of this book—especially the last three chapters—contain guidance and tools, but I do not presume to know *the* magic formula or any sort of step-by-step ritual. In addition to your own spirituality and practice, these tools are presented to help you better understand the demonic and ways of managing preternatural encounters.

Please note: To comfort those believing they are possessed, some prayers and rituals can be done in person as a type of reassurance; however, the vast majority of the work should take place in the privacy of the exorcist's home. The only exception to this would be a house cleansing, which obviously requires onsite intervention. Cleansing a dwelling doesn't carry the same liabilities as working with a human being.

Exorcism & Words of Warning

Claims of possession or demonic activity should always be

approached with the utmost skepticism. The likelihood of a person **not** being possessed is exponentially greater than an actual infestation. A legitimate demoniac will never ask to have the demon driven out of them. At no point in the Bible did anyone ever come to Jesus and explicitly state, "I'm demon possessed—please get it/them out of me." Even well meaning folks can do irreparable damage to the fragile psyche of one with a serious mental illness by entertaining satanic delusions.

The stereotypical, "traditional" Rite of Exorcism is outdated and dangerous. The legal, psychological, and ethical consequences far outweigh any perceived benefit. If for some reason you were to encounter an authentic demoniac, consider the following from the 19th chapter of The Acts of the Apostles (KJV):

> Then certain of the vagabond Jews, exorcists, took upon them to call over them which had evil spirits the name of the LORD Jesus, saying, We adjure you

> by Jesus whom Paul preacheth. And there were
> seven sons of one Sceva, a Jew, and chief of the
> priests, which did so. And the evil spirit answered
> and said, Jesus I know, and Paul I know; but who
> are ye? And the man in whom the evil spirit was
> leaped on them, and overcame them, and prevailed
> against them, so that they fled out of that house
> naked and wounded. (v. 13-16)

This is a sober warning. As practitioners, there is a natural tendency to want to help those who are suffering. Face-to-face exorcism is risky for all involved. A desire or whim to confront a potential demon or lower spirit is reckless. Outside of the Catholic Church, there is no accrediting body or formal credentialing process; however, those reading this book may feel a deep calling that is devoid of self-aggrandizement or the need to satisfy a sort of dark inquisitiveness.

At the same time, the aspiring demonologist is not an exorcist. The "exorcist in training" is not an exorcist. Those "fascinated" or "into" para-reality television, horror films, and ghosts are *not* exorcists. If anything I just said upset you or made you second-guess yourself, you are definitely not an exorcist.

Honoring the Past, Experiencing the Present

Just because something is older does not mean that it's necessarily better. An ancient text or practice may or may not have more validity than something modern (or vice versa); however, we have to honor our ancestors, learn from their experience, and place a healthy amount of trust in their guidance. Traditions do not exist for their own sake; we keep the ones alive that are worthwhile and add value or meaning to our lives. Others can be tossed aside or left for future generations to examine and determine their relevance within their lifetime.

Any magico-religious practice becomes toxic when it

leans into extremes, so we have to be careful in our balancing of tradition and experience. Heavy reliance on tradition can leave us stagnant, detached from The Practice. We are saying that our experience has no relevance, and the best has been discovered and used by those that came before us. On the other hand, we cannot entirely discount the establishment without regard for the past.

It's not unlike practicing medicine. New doctors come to medical school and find Grey's Anatomy on the required reading list. He may have lived and worked in the early part of the 19th Century, but his scholarship and the engravings that are the hallmark of his work are applicable today. His map of the human body is foundational in the study of anatomy and physiology.

Aspiring physicians do not start at ground zero; Henry Gray has the layout of the human body from a single cell to complex organs and systems already described in great detail with meticulous illustrations.

At the same time, it is critical (and required) for these students to explore a human cadaver to get a firsthand look for themselves. Dr. Gray did the foundational work; students use his work as a guide as they experientially explore human anatomy; and they use all of these as a starting point for their own eventual practice.

Likewise, we should honor the groundwork of practitioners before us. It may not be concrete science like anatomy, but it is still the basis for our initial rites and practices. As with medical school, we have our icons and starting points, but we have to see for ourselves and appropriate the things that work into our practice and dismiss the unfruitful or inaccurate. In other words, do what works, and leave the rest aside. What may have worked for one person at another time and place may not necessarily resonate with us. Respect your inner witness and instincts.

My strain of spiritual practice carries my maternal roots from 18th Century New Orleans and the mystique of the surrounding parishes, and my paternal beginnings are of a strict Catholic bent as practiced in 15th Century France. Both sides of my family converged into the northern part of the United States in the early 1900s. This was based on the opportunities of the Industrial Revolution and subsequent American Dream promised by the automotive industry. Our spiritual needs and practices changed with the so-called mainstream. Growing up in Pontiac, Michigan, my mother spent a lot of time at tent revivals. Although her family embraced Baptist teachings, these sawdust-on-the-floor, Holy Ghost-manifesting meetings on the outskirts of the city were a significant part of her childhood. My father was a confirmed Lutheran and married my mother in the Lutheran Church; however, both were quickly excommunicated once they began appearing at Sunday night meetings in small, Pentecostal churches.

Finally, my nuclear family settled into the full-blown, Charismatic, Pentecostal Movement along with the other "Jesus Freaks" of the 1960s and 70s. Spirit has been calling my family for centuries, and our response has varied by generation. While we are faithful to our foundational experiences, we also continue to examine and reframe our practices based on Shekinah's leading.

I became an ordained, non-denominational Christian minister in my early 20s; about a decade later, I took my vows/precepts as a Buddhist monk. While being part reverend and part monk, I also began attending "entity release" meetings in the home of a local Spiritualist and Medium. These meetings were but a trickle of the flashfloods and rivers to come. My appetite for the spiritual, the esoteric, and the occult was ravenous, and I refused to stop until I drilled deep enough to hit water.

Spirit knows us better than we know ourselves, and I am continually surprised at the various directions into which I am moved. Demonology and exorcism were never a personal passion for me, but the Great Cloud of Witnesses that continue to guide my path know me better than I know myself. Divinity draws us where we are needed most while providing us with the tools and knowledge to answer the proverbial call.

Keeping Things in Perspective
While an understanding of the demonic is important, it's not something upon which a healthy practice dwells. When we place too much emphasis on the darker side of spirituality, we actually attract these lower functioning entities to us.

Even if you don't feel like a "real" exorcist, you have the ability to privately and remotely confront the demonic if the situation arises. You should never seek out, invoke, or look for evil. It's out there, and it always bares its teeth when least expected.

As we wrap our thoughts and intentions in the cloak of Shekinah (as discussed in the fifth chapter), any demonic presence can be identified with calm detachment and with an assurance that they are powerless against our minds, homes, and loved ones. Invoking saints and performing other rituals can be applied as necessary to neutralize or drive away any negativity.

One last caution for supernatural tourists and paranormal dabblers: There are always dark entities that are more than willing to satisfy reckless curiosity at a very great expense. **You have been warned.**

✣ **Consider this...**

I have only encountered three authentic instances of demonic possession since my departure from the Pentecostal church. In one of these, the demon spoke through the man in a voice I can only describe as canine.

EXORCIST RISING

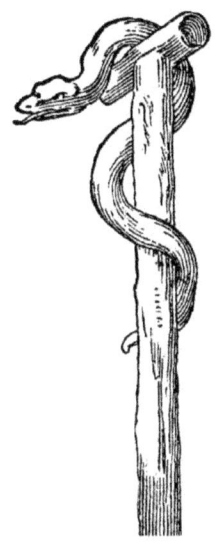

4 SERPENT SPEAK

And there appeared unto them cloven tongues like as of fire, and it sat upon each of them. And they were all filled with the Holy Ghost, and began to speak with other tongues, as the Spirit gave them utterance.

~Acts 2:3-4 (KJV)

From Azusa Street to Bourbon Street

My experience with the supernatural began in 1979. Before the emergence of self-proclaimed healers, psychics, televangelists, and demonologists, there was the Pentecostal Movement. As a little boy, I spent Sunday nights with my family at a little Pentecostal church in Pontiac, Michigan where the supernatural coexisted with the natural. To the spectator, this type of spirituality may have seemed "otherworldly," "strange," or even "crazy."

I witnessed real people with very real problems walk into this charged atmosphere and (literally) leave their diseases and demons behind. I witnessed the face of the schizophrenic as he came back into in his right mind, and I saw the countenance of the oppressed and possessed as it shifted from one of torment to one of freedom. I heard the voice of angels and saw the blue light of Shekinah.

EXORCIST RISING

My family and I were active believers *in* and practitioners *of* the most spiritually conspicuous denomination of Christianity in recent history. Throughout my childhood and teenage years, I experienced the supernatural on a weekly basis. Divine healing, speaking in "tongues of angels," prophecy, and even "driving out devils" (i.e. exorcism) were as typical as play dates and summer vacations.

Pentecostal Christianity emerged in 1906 during a three-year revival in Los Angeles. William J. Seymour held the first meeting at 312 Azusa Street on April 14, 1906.[11] It was a simple building with sawdust on the floors, but the manifestations of the divine were unlike anything seen in Christianity for nearly two millennia. Thousands were reported to have received "the Baptism of the Holy Ghost with the evidence of speaking in tongues." The raw power that manifested nightly terrified the surrounding area. Neighbors reported blasting or explosive sounds coming from the 312 address, and the fire department was called on several occasions to extinguish the glowing "cloud" or "flames" that rested on the flat, tarred roof.[12] The implied veil between the supernatural and the phenomenal world was nonexistent.

As an adult, I've seen and experienced this same type of hyper-reality in other denominations, cultures, and religions. I've felt it in the presence of His Holiness the 14th Dalai Lama in Indianapolis, at the tomb of Marie LaVeau in New Orleans' St Louis Cemetery #1, in the sanctuary of Queen of Angels Catholic Church in Chicago, in the Botanicas of Miami, and in "New Age" stores discreetly located throughout the Bible belt.

I've learned that no amount of academic research or philosophizing can replace the experiential. We can be guided by the writings of others—modern and ancient—but

---

[11] Owens, R.A. (2001). The Azusa Street Revival: The Pentecostal Movement begins in America. In V. Synan (Ed.) *The Century of the Holy Spirit: 100 years of Pentecostal and Charismatic renewal.* (p. 53) Nashville, TN: Thomas Nelson, Inc.
[12] Ibid.

we have to know for ourselves. For me, there is no question mark regarding the reality of the celestial, the angelic, and the demonic.

Anywhere we go, Spirit abounds.

Pente-Catho-Orleanism: An Integrated Approach
People always ask, "So, what are you?" I don't have a name for it. The best way to describe my practice is Pente-Catho-Orleanism, which is a combination of my Pentecostal beginnings, some of the Catholic sacramentals (not sacraments), and the magico-religious leanings of my personal "Promised Land": New Orleans, Louisiana. In no way do I suppose that my spirituality is exclusive or the best. My practice is based on my studies and experiences, but I know there are many truths to be learned from others. I'll continue to experience and seek until my time in this body has expired.

Finally, I do not subscribe to the notion that we need to learn the secret handshake of an elect few to be a worthy practitioner—it smacks of elitism (and frequently involves large sums of money implying one can buy their way into spiritual fulfillment and legitimacy). As the Buddha teaches, we need to "be a light unto ourselves," and "it is not gotten from another."

Some of the hallmarks of my magico-religious practice include the following:

> It is magick in the sense that certain accoutrements and rituals lend themselves to a desired outcome.

> It is religious in the sense that certain, culturally-comfortable/appropriate archetypes resonate with me. Specifically, my devotion is to The Blessed Virgin Mary, saints, and angels. I am deeply devoted to my "Celestial Helpers."

Experience and practice supersede affiliation or endorsement from so-called masters.

A hybrid of other religions is more effective than a homogeneous body of practice. Every religion has redeeming qualities and elements worthy of our learned consideration.

Celestial bodies, herbs, oils, words, and other proven tools have distinctive power and influence within spiritual realms.

We can glean from several sources and experiences and capitalize on the things that actually work for us. There is certain freedom when we are authentic in our dealings with the mystical that do not include the need for "thou shalt nots" and unnecessary morality-based rules. This authenticity keeps up spiritually vibrant—it makes us fully alive.

Establishing Your Practice

To operate *within* and to interact *with* the more subtle realms, we need a starting point. For some, this is nature, deities, a coven or gathering, an ancient text, or even this book. It can be a matter of trial and error, and what works for one person doesn't always work for another. We borrow, and we learn from those with the same esoteric or spiritual leanings, but most avoid adhering too closely to what others claim to be "The Truth." When we resign our common sense and internal cues to the ideologies of a group or person, we're handing over our free will. We are thinking, sensing, knowing beings, and we don't need another person telling us we're nothing without them. This is fertile ground for cult activity and further distancing from our authentic path. A healthy practice is evident when it consists of the following characteristics or "seals." Although there may be some redundancy here, it's essential and worthy of repeating.

Informed
It's important to be well read about many traditions, religions, and practices. Dismissing an idea without any sort of examination or study is irresponsible. An advanced practitioner knows the origins behind several systems or methodologies to gain perspective. Without several reference points, we are unable to articulate exactly why we are on our chosen path.

Eclectic
The most significant benefit of examining the findings of others is that it leads us into unexpected directions. When we are open and willing to listen to others, we often take nuggets of truth away from such interactions. If you only excavate in one location, you're missing the opportunity for other gems. We begin to build a treasure-trove of techniques and energies that would not have revealed themselves otherwise.

Experiential
It's a grievous error to take someone's words at face value. Just because a manuscript is ancient does not mean that it's reliable or even truthful. Just because a certain spiritual figure sells out arenas they should not be given a free pass. We should embrace things that work for us—things that *we* know to be true. There is no book or sage that can replace the power of direct experience. When we have an encounter, we gain authentic understanding. This understanding is the result of something that yields the desired result and carries an energy that personally elevates us.

Autonomous

Whether we choose to practice in a more solitary setting or within a group, a healthy measure of independence is essential. Certain growth comes through interaction with others of a similar disposition; still, our practice is more dynamic when it is grounded in our individuality.

Celestial Helpers

Our world is filled with entities—personal and impersonal, and we can learn to work with these eager participants in ways that will supercharge our practice. They have been venerated and approximated in culturally relevant forms throughout history. The most obvious of these is The Goddess. She has assumed the forms and names of Our Lady of Guadalupe, Kali, Isis, Baba Yaga, Kwan Yin, Athena, Diana, The Virgin Mary, Demeter, Yemayah, Coatlique, and countless others. Nobody has an exclusive on "It," and we have the freedom to invoke and worship in any manner of our choosing. My magico-religious practice contains many elements of what others would call Mariolatry[13] or something akin to the Marialis Cultus[14] of the Middle Ages.

The Exorcist Rises

To help those under demonic attack, you do not have to fly to another country, go through an initiation, have some stamp of approval by any particular leader, be of a certain ethnicity, or any other such nonsense. This is part of the trappings of traditional religion. Feelings of worthiness and belonging supersede a true relationship with the Divine.

---

[13] A heretical form of devotion to the Virgin Mary as forbidden by the Catholic Church

[14] The Medieval European practice of Marian Worship and other rites contrary to those "approved" by the Catholic Church

One cannot teach a person to be of a certain spiritual caliber anymore than one can teach them to be nice. If you bought this book (or are browsing through it at a bookstore), you have already demonstrated your willingness to consider other paths and approaches. As mentioned before, the Practice is based on experience. If it works, nobody can convince you otherwise. If it does not, perhaps this isn't the right path for you.

The nuanced specifics of precisely how an exorcist operates is a bit vague and secret for several reasons. One of these is to protect our inner sanctum; we do not want to cast our proverbial pearls before the swine. Ignorance and bigotry breed contempt, fear, and hate. The primal, visceral nature of the ageless battle between light and dark is easily misunderstood as a 'nonsense,' 'evil,' 'archaic,' or even 'savage.' Like a book of shadows or family tradition, it is intended for the sincere. It does not have mass appeal, and I hope it never does. The general malaise of humanity in its current state tends to lend itself to the comfortable, the familiar. A sermon or homily, few hymns, and a wall plaque of "Footprints in the Sand" suit most folks just fine.

Exorcism is a practice of the (seemingly) downtrodden, the misunderstood, the forgotten, and the 'peculiar.' It is the best kept secret of the ones that call on the names of the oldest spiritual forces in the universe. While the masses do their weekly time at a church without a change of heart, mind, or a spiritual experience beyond thinking of their 'sin,' those engaged in the ancient arts are transported into celestial realms where miracles are possible and the power is palpable. We have an intimacy with the Divine, a mystical marriage that does not need the blessing of a priest or the approval of a board of elders. We are not servants; rather, we are the beloved. We find an authenticity free of contingencies and dogmatic baggage. Our sighs and whispered intentions become more than reflexive. Like Native American Mystic and Healer, Black Elk, we find ourselves saying: "And when I breathed, my breath was lightning." We are empowered, sure of our experience, liberated, and free.

Putting It All Together

Regardless of your methodology, only you know if you are capable of spiritual warfare. The real work of magico-religious practice (including exorcism or spirit binding) is one of healing, of liberation. If you been granted the faith, confidence, ability, and experience, who are you to withhold it from those in need? No sanction from an organized religion is required to do good. No ecclesiastical approval is needed to intercede on behalf of those that cannot help themselves. My experience affirms the words of Jesus as recorded in the Gospel of Mark, chapter 16 (KJV):

> And these signs shall follow them that believe; In my name shall they cast out devils; they shall speak with new tongues;
>
> They shall take up serpents; and if they drink any deadly thing, it shall not hurt them; they shall lay hands on the sick, and they shall recover. (v. 17-18).

5 THE NEWER RITE

Therefore we, before him bending, this great Sacrament revere; types and shadows have their ending, for The Newer Rite is here.

~St. Thomas Aquinas, 13th Century

 The Newer Rite is a non-dogmatic approach to exorcizing demonic entities. Unlike the (Catholic) Roman Ritual, it is not a prescribed collection of prayers to be performed in a certain order by church appointed individuals. The formulaic is replaced with the organic, and the tools and prayers are as varied as the types and severity of any (potential) diabolical infestation. The pages that follow may be read sequentially, but the contents **are not** intended to be used in the order presented.

Please think of these as prospective tools and resources. They may be used individually (e.g. placing the Jubilee Medal of St. Benedict between a mattress and box springs) or in any combination of your choosing (e.g. fixing/dressing a novena candle with suitable oils and reciting a particular Psalm). There is no wrong approach, per se, but it is critical to understand the rationale and symbolism of what you choose to implement.

It is my hope and intention that Shekinah rests on each readers and grants them spiritual discernment and the divine wisdom to liberate all that are afflicted.

The Power: Plugging Into The Divine

The Blessed Virgin Mary (BVM)
It's important to understand and operate within Spirit when confronting the demonic. Despite our best intentions, our work requires something even greater than willpower or passion. It requires The Divine. One of the more familiar manifestations of this can be found in the Blessed Virgin Mary as the Queen of Heaven.

Each "version" of The Virgin Mary has various attributes. When we invoke or channel The Holy Mother using a specific name such as Our Lady of Guadalupe, we need to know what we're asking for. As with electricity, there are currents that move at various rates and with different intensities. With each, we can expect differing experiences and subsequent outcomes. For example, rituals involving Our Lady of Lourdes generate a gentle, warming sensation while the more severe energies of Our Lady of Fatima have the potential to overwhelm or frighten novices, which makes it especially important to be aware of the raw power that accommodates this type of work.

Regardless of the name we invoke, the nature of the power is still the same—there is no deviation from the actual source. At the same time, names and manifestations cannot be separated from this source. Each is the sound, the power, and the representation. The title "Queen of Heaven," the utterance of the words "Queen of Heaven," and the cosmic force known as the "Queen of Heaven" are inextricable. When we work with one, we are working with the other. All work in concert with our needs and requests within the matrix of our spiritual selves. Like a circuit board, we can release, direct, and harness the "electricity" being channeled.

Kundalini

Because we are divine, we already possess a certain measure of The Holy Mother's power. Our intentions and occult abilities lie dormant unless we learn to awaken and use them in creative ways. In Hindu and "New Age" traditions, this potential energy is called Kundalini, and it is likened to a coiled serpent located at the base of our spine. We can stir our natural abilities and cause Kundalini to rise up within us. The "snake" of our Kundalini ascends and opens our various power centers (i.e. chakras) to bring heightened awareness and the ability to "read" people, skillfully divine the future, and the capability to interact with the "dead" and other spiritual entities.

It's a hardly a coincidence that the serpent is a symbol for Kundalini. The Cosmic Mother is known as the one who treads on snakes—even crushes their heads. Many representations of the BVM include a writing snake at her feet. The implication is that she has dominion over the

Kundalini within each of us. She gently guides us through the process of developing our spiritual gifts and rising from our lowest selves into the more celestial realms. Saint Patrick is known to have driven serpents out of Ireland, which makes him another ally for working with potential energy just waiting to be awakened and activated within each of us.

Shekinah/The Holy Ghost
Shekinah Glory was a part of my Charismatic Pentecostal Christian vernacular, but it was used in reference to manifestations of the Holy Ghost (i.e. the third "man" of the Holy Trinity). Interestingly, the term is never mentioned directly in the Bible, which we deemed the only "true and complete Word of God." I was exceptionally surprised to learn that Yah Shekinah, Shekinah Glory, or Shekinah (pronounced "shah-KI-nuh"—the "ki" rhymes with "eye") is rooted in the oral tradition of Kabbalah. This form of Ancient Jewish Mysticism is a departure from the Torah and the laws of Moses—it assumes more of a magical than a dogmatic approach to spirituality. Shekinah is the part of the Mystical Body of God that interacts with humanity and grants access to higher realms and entities as in the Azusa Street Revival and on the Day of Pentecost.

Shekinah does not have a proper name. In the Judeo-Christian faith, the Father is known by many names including Jehovah, YHVH, and I AM. The Son also has several (e.g. Jesus, Yeshua, and Emmanuel), but the Holy Ghost/Shekinah transcends names. Description and metaphor attempt to explain this Presence, but it cannot be defined. In the New Testament, it ascended on Jesus "like a dove" and appeared during Pentecost "as a mighty rushing wind" in serpentine "tongues of fire." Words aren't adequate—just an attempted approximation.

In my experience, this is the most overwhelming manifestation of the Divine. While the intensity or "thickness" varies, this is the least subtle of celestial energies.

It is an atmosphere that is unmistakable. When it[15] manifests, there is no question as to its authenticity. The air in the room literally becomes alive with a tangible weight along the lines of extreme humidity just before a storm. Unlike a pre-storm atmosphere, breathing takes *less* effort, and there is no sweating or discomfort.

Within this intelligent field of living power, anything is possible. Many (myself included) have seen it as a blue light, and others report seeing "a gold color." Still, others perceive it as a luminescent fog or mist—sometimes emitting what looks like small charges of lightning. What pilots and seafarers commonly call St. Elmo's Fire is actually Shekinah protecting them in inclement weather or in situations of potential disaster.

The first experience I had with Shekinah as an adult took place in a small, nondescript church in Cass City, Michigan. During that temperate March evening, I noticed myself becoming caught up in the music. The small congregation of about 35 people suddenly became a harmonious, singular voice. The bass guitar, the lead guitar, the piano, the drums, and the percussive sound of the tambourine shifted somehow. As a group, we thought we were singing the music, but the music started singing us.

It was warm, loving, exciting, and there was no trace of discomfort or fear of any kind. The bass pierced and pulsed like thunder, and the air in the room thickened with an anticipation of something great about to happen. I was suddenly spellbound, silently vibrating within what I would describe as a type of living mist. Everything was bathed in blue—the pastor, the congregation, the musicians, and my awareness faded into the glorious light of it.

After this experience, I was told that I moved from my pew, into the aisle, and to front of the small altar area. With eyes closed, I assumed a contorted/hunched position, face forward, and commenced in a sort of tribal dance. It was

---

[15] While Shekinah is female, "she" is also the third "man" of the Holy Trinity. "It" has been used by the author for the sake of simplicity.

described to me as "a Native American war dance." In reality, I was painfully shy, never danced in my life, and I did everything I could to keep myself out of the limelight. I was told I had been filled with the Holy Ghost, baptized in fire. "I" was not there. We were singing a simple, repetitive song, but the words carried a mystical intonation I had not anticipated. As I sang, the doorway of my spirit was blown wide open.

It is The Power that creates, sustains, heals, and consumes. It is the antidote to any illness, possession, curse, demonic attachment, or supernatural attack. Shekinah is both gentle and fierce, and She must be experienced rather than discussed or understood.

All forms of exorcism and healing are predicated on the manifestation of Shekinah. For a true practitioner, She is the supreme light that shines into and through all things living and all things inanimate. Without Shekinah, we can do nothing.

NOAH TYSICK

The Home Altar: Your Supernatural Workbench

There are entire books devoted to this topic. Altars are something very personal—a sacred point of contact. The first alter I ever created was extremely simple. I was just finishing my bachelor's degree, and I read a few books about meditation. I didn't have a lot of money at the time, but I wanted a designated space away from my usual surroundings. I took a simple end table and placed it in a spare bedroom. I chose items very carefully—saint candles from the local dollar store, a chaplet and rosary given to me as a Christmas gift from my parents, a small box containing letters from family and friends that had encouraged me in the past, and a small figure of the elephant-headed "remover of obstacles" (i.e. Hinduism's Ganesha).

The monetary investment was minimal, but I had a space to chant, meditate, and pray. It became a place for me to "officially" separate myself from school, work, and other obligations to turn my focus inward. As Shekinah manifested within me, each object on my altar became infused with the juju of hours spent in practice. My knowledge *of* and love *for* The Divine developed significantly in this humble corner of my little apartment. The altar was deceptively simple to any onlooker, but it brought me closer to Spirit in ways that I can't adequately summarize here. Fifteen years have passed, and my altar has evolved into several different ones. Some are simple; others are very elaborate, but the purpose is the same.

Erecting an Altar

Your altar is an outward indication of your inner intentions; it's where the physical and the supernatural intersect, which is why the personal altar is a necessity. It is your spiritual sanctuary and workplace.

About eighty percent of the work you do to bind and cast out the demonic happens in the privacy of your sacred space. It doesn't have to be fancy or cost a lot of money, but it should be representative of your path and commitment. Common items include statues, books, framed images, prayer cards, incense burners, prayer beads—anything that puts you in a positive space will do. Don't worry about doing it "right;" just designate a corner, closet, or entire room and begin to personalize it. Be creative, colorful, and don't worry about getting the best objects before getting it set up. The important part is to create it and begin spending time in front of it. Additional objects, details and embellishments will come with time.

Choose Your Patron

Maybe you feel drawn to a certain saint or Hindu deity; perhaps, you find yourself empowered by a particular religious leader or mythological image. The best way to begin an altar is to choose a patron, make him/her the centerpiece, and add other elements around your chosen Cosmic Helper.

As with any friend, it's important to develop a relationship through spending time at the altar making daily offerings (e.g. incense, candles, food, and drink). Your patron is not a genie that's there to do your bidding, nor is he or she only to be honored when you need something.

Your altar is a constant reminder of their living presence. Again, you don't have to be rich or spend a lot of money to show your love, but a clean, maintained altar keeps the relationship alive. As you encounter difficult circumstances, you'll naturally approach your beloved with any petitions for help. Because of the ongoing relationship, asking for support is appropriate. If you only come when you need something, your request may not be granted.

Over time, your practice will deepen and other statues and icons will make their way onto your altar, which is a good thing. As a 21st Century Practitioner, this may also include deities of other religions. Maybe you're drawn to a Hindu god or goddess, or perhaps you feel drawn to an entity of Buddhist or Egyptian origin. **There is no wrong approach or expression of The Power.** Shekinah manifests in innumerable ways, and different saints, entities, or manifestations of the BVM[16] are representative of Her various attributes. Don't limit yourself.

> The altar is where The Newer Rite of Exorcism begins and ends. It does not involve a face-to-face showdown in which a person is exorcised in the traditional sense. Preparatory acts like prayer and fasting should be conducted before any meeting. Subsequent magico-religious work also happens in the sanctity of the practitioner's own space.

---

[16] BVM is a common abbreviation used to reference the Blessed Virgin Mary

The Nature of the Demonic

Western culture in general and early American Puritanism in particular created an atmosphere of hyper-vigilance and hyper-sensitivity to witches, demons, and the like. If a settlement suffered any sort of hardship, the automatic response was to look for the unholy cause. A "witch" had to be identified and destroyed to protect the public from further (so-called) demonic attacks.

Even as a modern society, it isn't difficult to slip into the tendency to find a devil under every rock or at the root of every misfortune. Contrary to our ancestors, the tendency should be to rule out all natural explanations before even entertaining the idea of the supernatural or preternatural. Technology, medicine, pharmacology, and other advancements have changed our understanding of the inner workings of the mind, and it is essential that we don't digress into silly superstition. Common sense is our greatest weapon.

Despite the misinformation regarding the evil and demonic of past centuries, we can glean worthwhile information from some of these early expositions of demonology. A 17th Century text entitled *The Certainty of the World of Spirits* provides us with significant insight into the behavior of demonic entities. The author states,

> Devils have a greater Game to play invisibly, then by Apparitions. O happy World, if they do not do a hundred thousand times more hurt [by not showing themselves]![17]

---

[17] Baxter, R. (1691). *The Certainty of the World of the Spirits*. Available from http://ebooks.library.cornell.edu/cgi/t/text/text-idx?c=witch;idno=wit012

Silence and subtlety serve demons well. They are exceptionally difficult to discern for this and a few other reasons:

1. Along with our "enlightened" advancements, we have assumed a more extreme disbelief in their existence than previous civilizations.
2. They capitalize on the above by operating subtly, invisibly, and as discreetly as possible.
3. When a person attempts to find or expose an authentic demonic possession, obsession, infestation, etc., the entity will attempt to hide itself even more than if you weren't looking for it.

They have nothing to prove, yet they torment hearts and minds without mercy and without regard for social or economic status. As agents of evil, their objectives are horrifically simple. They are hardwired to do the following according to The Gospel of St. Mark:

Kill
This is not literal, of course, but they can cause people to harm themselves. Aside from self-mutilation, self-destructive behaviors, and suicidal tendencies, the demonic deplete victims of all hope. They strip-mine the psyche of any sense of well-being.

Steal
This can include physical and material wealth, but the higher aim is to deprive, to dehumanize. The Satanic takes things that cannot be restored (like innocence).

Destroy
Low spirits are bottomless, ravenously hungry and will attack and assail until nothing remains. They "eat"

EXORCIST RISING

indiscriminately and endlessly.[18] Demons divide families, devastate lives—nothing is off-limits.

If a spirit causes confusion, torment, or incites any of the above, it is very likely demonic. While these descriptions are relatively broad in nature, they provide a reasonable rubric from which we can begin to determine what is natural and what is preternatural.

---

[18] See the tenth chapter of the Gospel of St. John (V. 10)

Types of Demonic Activity

The most well-known and rarest type of demonic assault is **possession**. Minus the Hollywood effects, this is when a demonic spirit lives within an individual. The rational mind and personality are overtaken, and the demon usurps the faculties of the victim for its own purposes.

Obsession is relatively common, and it involves a person with an unnatural preoccupation with the Satan(ism), torture, murder, and all things dark. While a possessed person can become obsessed, an obsessed person is not necessarily possessed. Depending on the circumstances, obsession is most likely a mental health issue that requires medical attention. While the person may be unpleasant or even downright scary to be around, they aren't typically dangerous. The right professional treatment(s) can provide the individual with a healthier worldview that doesn't dwell on the dark and the macabre.

Oppression is the most common form of demonic attack, and it can happen to virtually anyone. It is not a sign that a person is evil, nor is it indicative of any wrongdoing on the part of the host. Oppression is a form of spiritual torment or tyranny in which a person is a target of sorts. The entity assails the victim with physical, mental, and spiritual torments that lack any sort of natural explanation. To be clear, nothing demonic has taken over the body or faculties of the tormented—there is no change *in* or deviation *from* their normal behavior. "Binding" or healing, rather than exorcism proper, can release the person from the entity and any subsequent attacks.

Attachment is a form of oppression, which can impact human beings, inanimate objects, and locations (e.g. homes, property, entire cities, etc.). Attachment is based on a territorial claim in which the entity feels it has the right of ownership over a person, group, home, city, or object. The cause of this type of infestation can be generational, and divination may be used to determine the cause. Yet again, this **does not include the indwelling of a person,** but an exorcism of the host—animate or inanimate—is required.

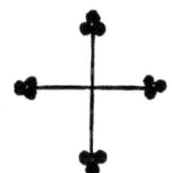

Cleromancy: Casting the Cowries

The process of determining potential demonic activity, possible causes, and methods by which to drive the evil out isn't always clear. The newer generation of exorcists understand the need to exhaust all natural explanations and solutions prior to applying any magico-religious work to the situation.

In addition to assistance of our Celestial Helpers,

meditation, and prayer, divination can be an effective tool. Typically, "divination" stirs up spooky images of ancient people examining the internal organs of an animal to determine a course of action or to foretell future events. The type of divination I'm referencing is simply using an intermediary object to discern what Spirit would have us do. Seeking divine guidance by "casting lots" is not the evil practice some would claim it to be. Cleromancy is often used in New Orleanian magico-religious practices, and it is simply used to get a yes/no answer from Spirit.

While there are several Biblical references that forbid any type of soothsaying and divination, there are nearly an equal number of references in which Levite priests and others use "casting lots" to divine the will of God. One particular tool was the Urim and Thummim kept within the breastplate of Aaron and other ancient Jewish priests.[19] They were used to determine which animals would be sacrificed and which would be let free (i.e. the scapegoat), to determine guilt or innocence, and to assign parcels of land.

Many New Orleanian practitioners use cowry shells in the same way. The open side—known as the "mouth of the gods"—gives an affirmative or 'yes' answer when cast and

---

[19] Exodus 28:30, Leviticus 8:8

facing up. A 'no' is indicated when the opening lands facedown. A single shell can be used for cleromancy, but it is more common to use four or even sixteen at a time. The more upward 'mouths' showing when the cowries are cast, the more favorable the answer and vice-versa.

Some practitioners would like people to think that some sort of exclusive initiation or instruction is required to effectively cast the cowries, but this is simply not true. Unfortunately, these types of claims are made in an attempt to 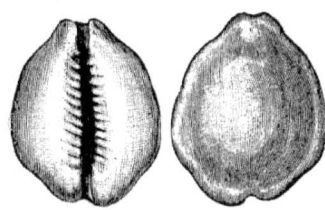 collect sums of money from those that are unfamiliar with the practice. The reality is that anyone desiring to use the cowries can quickly learn what Spirit is saying using the position, direction, various patterns, and upward/downward facing of the shells. The conversation is between yourself and the Divine—there's no wrong way to do it. The more you use your shells, the more connected you become with Spirit. Your ability to discern the right course of action develops exponentially with repeated use.

Below are some sample questions that can be used as a starting point for casting the cowries. Remember, to ask questions that can be answered with a 'yes' or 'no.'

- Is this situation the result of a demonic attack?
- Is the attack in the form of oppression?
- Is the attack psychological?
- Should I invoke St. _____ against this entity?
- Should I also use a Psalm in this case?
- Would Psalm __ be the most effective?
- Is the client being deceptive (i.e. Am I only getting part of the story)?

Chirothesy: Laying on of Hands

Chirothesy is a foreign concept to many. Some see it as a hokey tool of televangelists to add drama to their act; others see it as something reserved for popes and high-ranking religious officials. "Laying hands" on someone (as it's commonly called) is not specific to the West, nor is it something that requires anything more than faith and intention.

The purpose of this practice is one of transference. When we place our hands on someone that is ill or demonically oppressed, we are creating a circuit of sorts. The practitioner lives with a certain measure of Shekinah resting on and within their person. By blessing or praying over another while touching them on the forehead or afflicted body part, The Power is channeled like water through a trench into the thirsty spirit of the person in need. Because Shekinah is never diminished, the one that is healing does not feel depleted. In fact, this Living Presence begins to self-propagate as the afflicted becomes more receptive.

As a teenager, I suffered with (what I would later learn were) ulcers. I felt that telling someone about the pain would show that I was a nervous. I didn't want to be known as an anxious person, and I kept up my façade for several years. During one particular bout of excruciating pain in the upper part of my stomach, I was in a church service.

My pastor at the time opened the altar for prayer. He asked anyone that needed healing to come forward to allow God to touch their bodies and minds. I went to the front of the church along with several other folks, but I did not tell the pastor or anyone else why I needed prayer.

As I closed my eyes and asked for relief from anxiety and the stabbing pain in my stomach, someone came from behind me and placed one hand on the front of my stomach and one on the back. It was one of our church elders, and her hands were touching the <u>exact</u> location of the pain. As we prayed within the atmosphere of the Holy Ghost, I could feel a warming flow of electricity that seemed to be growing in intensity. The Power that rested on her was flowing in a circular current that passed from her hand, though my stomach, back into her other hand, and back around again. The torrent of Shekinah became so intense, it began to envelop the both of us—within, without, around, and through.

The woman and I didn't speak before she felt led to pray for me in this way, and we didn't discuss it after. Spirit knew my need and delivered it through a willing conduit. My stomach was whole for the first time in years, my anxiety lifted for the time being. There was no dramatic exchange or sideshow element to the healing that took place. It was the compassion of another following the ebb and flow of Shekinah to deliver the relief I was too proud to seek for myself.

Through meditation and daily magico-religious practice, you may find yourself laying hands on someone instinctively. You may even find it appropriate to bless yourself with this sacred practice. Chirothesy can be used to bless, heal, and direct the flow of Shekinah. The transference of power strengthens both the channeler and the recipient.

> ✷ Consider this...
>
> ```
> If you lay hands on someone or
> something that is inhabited by or
> attached to an unclean spirit, you
> can't "catch it." Even if there is
> resistance from the other side, you
> are protected by Shekinah in you.
> ```

Holy Water

All water is holy in the sense that it is revered on some level in all cultures and religions. Even those who do not consider themselves spiritual know the power and importance of water—very literally, it is a main component of living tissue and a continuous supply is mandatory for survival. At an even deeper level, the implications go beyond physical need. Water is *the* universal elixir used for cleansing, baptizing, and blessing. It is more than a liturgical prop, and it is a necessity for any type of exorcism or healing.

The main question for any practitioner is: What separates the holy or magical from 'regular' water? This isn't easily answered, as it depends on the individual using it. For some, authentic holy water is the product of tap water being blessed by a Catholic Priest. Others claim mystical sources from nature rather than a person. The Ganges River is sacred to Hindus, and the miracle spring at Lourdes, France emanates directly from the spot where the Blessed Mother appeared to Saint Bernadette. Regardless of your preference, water should be used when expelling a demonic entity. You may wish to bless yourself with a light sprinkling, or you can sprinkle water on an object or within a space—there's no wrong way of doing it.

Aside from buying holy water from a shrine, through an online religious goods site, or by filling a container at the nearest Catholic Church, there are several applicable ways in which practitioners can make their own. Blessing the water can be a simple, heartfelt intonation, or it can be done using one of the following established blessings.

Traditional Rite for Providing Holy Water 1
God our Father, your gift of water brings life and freshness to the earth; it washes away our sins and brings us eternal life. We ask you now to bless ✝ this water, and to give us your protection on this day which you have made your own. Renew the living spring of your life within us and protect us in spirit and body, that we may be free from sin and come into your presence to receive your gift of salvation.

Traditional Rite for Providing Holy Water 2
Lord God almighty, creator of all life, of body and soul, we ask you to bless ✝ this water: as we use it in faith forgive our sins and save us from all illness and the power of evil. Lord, in your mercy give us living water, always springing up as a fountain of salvation: free us, body and soul, from every danger, and admit us to your presence in purity of heart.

Ancient Rite for Providing House Cleansing Water
Ancient Kabbalistic blessing of water was specifically done as a medium to expel demonic entities from a home or other building. The practitioner should place his/her hands over the vessel of water and chant the 10th Psalm nine times in a row (Optional: One drop of extra virgin olive oil may be added for every two ounces of water). Once blessed in this manner, the water or water/oil mixture can be sprinkled throughout the dwelling.[20]

> Why standest thou afar off, O LORD? why hidest thou thyself in times of trouble?
>
> The wicked in his pride doth persecute the poor: let them be taken in the devices that they have imagined. For the wicked boasteth of his heart's desire, and blesseth the covetous, whom the

---

[20] Trachtenberg, J. (1939). *Jewish magic and superstition: a study in folk religion.* (pp. 158-159) New York: Behrman's Jewish Book House.

NOAH TYSICK

LORD abhorreth. The wicked, through the pride of his countenance, will not seek after God: God is not in all his thoughts.

His ways are always grievous; thy judgments are far above out of his sight: as for all his enemies, he puffeth at them. He hath said in his heart, I shall not be moved: for I shall never be in adversity. His mouth is full of cursing and deceit and fraud: under his tongue is mischief and vanity. He sitteth in the lurking places of the villages: in the secret places doth he murder the innocent: his eyes are privily set against the poor. He lieth in wait secretly as a lion in his den: he lieth in wait to catch the poor: he doth catch the poor, when he draweth him into his net. He croucheth, and humbleth himself, that the poor may fall by his strong ones. He hath said in his heart, God hath forgotten: he hideth his face; he will never see it.

Arise, O LORD; O God, lift up thine hand: forget not the humble. Wherefore doth the wicked contemn God? he hath said in his heart, Thou wilt not require it. Thou hast seen it; for thou beholdest mischief and spite, to requite it with thy hand: the poor committeth himself unto thee; thou art the helper of the fatherless. Break thou the arm of the wicked and the evil man: seek out his wickedness till thou find none.

The LORD is King for ever and ever: the heathen are perished out of his land. LORD, thou hast heard the desire of the humble: thou wilt prepare their heart, thou wilt cause thine ear to hear: To judge the fatherless and the oppressed, that the man of the earth may no more oppress.

Optional Addition of Salt to Any Water Blessing

Using cleromancy or if led by Spirit, you can add salt to the already blessed water (≈one pinch/ounce of water). Before mixing the two, salt should be blessed. The following can be used for this purpose.

Almighty God, we ask you to bless ✚ this salt as once you blessed the salt scattered over the water by the prophet Elisha. Wherever this salt and water are sprinkled, drive away the power of evil and protect us always by the presence of the Holy Ghost.

Holy Fire

Effective magico-religious practice includes using fire even more than water, but many do not understand the full implications of what this truly means. In addition to lighting novena candles and saying prayers to the saints, there is also the misunderstood fire of Pentecost that many have not sought or received. The latter refers to Shekinah not only resting on your methods and practice but the personal indwelling of Shekinah. Plainly stated, She desires to speak through us with a power and authority that we would not have otherwise.

Setting the Lights

The act of lighting a candle is more than setting a mood or adding beauty to our homes. The igniting of a flame becomes a mystical undertaking when we combine it with a specific intention. In the New Orleanian tradition, this is called "Setting the Lights."

This process can be as simple or elaborate as one chooses. Typically, glass novena candles are used for this purpose. Choosing, dressing, and using candles for a desired outcome is a powerful supplement to a house cleansing or exorcism. It can be done as a preparatory or follow-up practice, which is a way of clarifying your intentions, seeking supernatural assistance, or sealing any subsequent ritual.

You have probably seen the type of candle I'm referencing in the ethnic food section of your local market. They're glass with an open top, and there is a label with a picture of the Blessed Mother, Jesus, or a Saint. The back label usually includes a recommended prayer. For a better selection of novena or vigil candles, you can check your local yellow pages for a religious supply store (Catholic), occult store, or a botanica. If you don't mind the extra cost of shipping there are numerous online vendors.

As referenced a bit later, most saints have at least one color that is associated with them. Plain candles in that color or any white candle are acceptable substitutes (i.e. those without religious markings or labels). Magico-religious work is always more effective if you choose a saint or color that applies to your intention. If you're not sure who to invoke, always default to white or any candle of the Queen of Heaven (e.g. Our Lady of Guadalupe, Our Lady of Grace, the Immaculate Heart of Mary, etc.). Based on my experience and practice, here is a brief list of candle colors that I have used to combat demonic entities. This list is not exhaustive, but you may find it a helpful starting point when you are setting lights.

> **Red:** Spiritual warfare, divine retribution, St. Michael, the Sacred Heart of Jesus, and the Precious Blood of Jesus. Use judiciously and reserve for difficult cases.
>
> **Orange:** In my experience, orange isn't entirely appropriate or effective in working against dark entities.
>
> **Yellow:** Indicates new beginnings in the spirit and psyche. Very effective for demonic obsession.
>
> **Green:** Restoration, abundance, St. Patrick, against substance abuse and self-destructive behavior.
>
> **Blue:** Shekinah, healing, Blessed Mother, angelic protection, against all forms of demonic activity. Strongly recommended.
>
> **Purple/Violet:** House cleansing/blessing. Against anxiety, depression, psychiatric and spiritual attacks, demonic possession of people, locations, and objects. Very powerful color for exorcism.
>
> **Black:** Not recommended.
>
> **White:** All purpose. For use in any situation.

Tongues of Angels and of Fire

There is a lot of controversy surrounding what is known as "speaking in tongues." As documented during the Azusa Street Revival and throughout the New Testament, the Holy Ghost—Shekinah manifested—descends on and into the willing. Without getting into an exegesis of scripture, I would like to reference three historical mentions of the supernatural ability to speak in celestial languages (sometimes called "tongues of angels"):

> And when the day of Pentecost was fully come, they were all with one accord in one place. And suddenly there came a sound from heaven as of a rushing mighty wind, and it filled all the house where they were sitting. And there appeared unto them cloven tongues like as of fire, and it sat upon each of them. And they were all filled with the Holy Ghost, and began to speak with other tongues, as the Spirit gave them utterance. (Acts 2:1-4, KJV)

> And these signs shall follow them that believe; In my name shall they cast out devils; they shall speak with new tongues […] (Mark 16:17, KJV)

> Likewise the Spirit also helpeth our infirmities: for we know not what we should pray for as we ought: but the Spirit itself maketh intercession for us with groanings which cannot be uttered. (Romans 8:26, KJV)

What do these passages tell us? 1. Shekinah has and still is speaking through people. 2. The new language is not necessarily one that humans can understand or classify. 3. Spirit speaks on our behalf in ways we cannot comprehend.

This very belief and practice is one reason there are so many denominations of Christianity. Speaking in Tongues isn't something practiced by the mainstream, and it is often mocked by outsiders. More importantly, I have experienced the initial descent and subsequent ability to pray, chant, sing in the way described in biblical references. It is not something you can learn, nor is it something you can fake. When Shekinah manifests within me, my celestial language is able to adequately communicate the unspeakable. At other times, I may not have the ability to ask for something in the appropriate manner, and Speaking in Tongues is Spirit's way of communicating through me and on my behalf.

As a practitioner and exorcist, the tendency to be formulaic at all times is strong; however, I can attest to the reality and efficacy of authentic celestial communication. On occasion, it may be appropriate to do so in a public forum, but it is mainly used during solitary times in meditation and prayer in front of my altar.

There are religious fanatics that try to usurp Speaking in Tongues as something reserved for the "holy" and the "elect," but I can assure you that spiritual spontaneity and receptivity are the prerequisites. I strongly recommend seeking the initial experience of being "baptized with fire" and the resulting ability to pray, exorcise demons, and heal others. If you seek it, you will find it.

More Essential Exorcism Tools

Each practitioner has a standard "toolbox" of items they use on a regular basis. Some of these objects are common and relatively easy to obtain; others may be a bit more obscure. While I cannot provide you with an exhaustive list of "ingredients" or accoutrements I utilize (that's an entirely separate book), I can touch on a small sampling of things Spirit has led me to use. Depending on your spiritual or religious leanings, other objects may resonate more with you. For our purposes here, I'm including those specific to my Pente-Catho-Orleanist roots.

Cross v. Crucifix

People frequently use these terms interchangeably, but they are far from synonymous. A cross is a simple symbol containing two intersecting lines—usually, the vertical is a bit longer. Regardless of embellishments or other markings, a cross is a general symbol of (Protestant) Christianity. It represents the risen Christ, victory, and the hope of eternal life.

A crucifix is a cross with a figure of Christ attached. This figure or corpus is what distinguishes a basic cross from a crucifix. The emphasis is on the passion and suffering of Jesus and the potency of the shedding of his Most Precious Blood.

When choosing a crucifix, there is another distinct feature practitioners should consider: Is his head raised, or is it lowered (i.e. either directly in front or to one side)? This may seem a bit pedantic, but the implications are worthy of consideration. If the head is raised, the crucifix represents the Christ mid-execution—suffering, tormented. He is literally at the crossroads between life and death—victim and victor. If the head is lowered, the crucifix signifies completion, atonement, surrender. It is the point at which Jesus left his earthly incarnation to descend into Hell. He is postmortem and pre-resurrection.

Of the three symbols just described, you can select the most appropriate for your purposes. There is no 'wrong' choice, but it's good to be intimately aware of the tools being used. When you consciously choose your instruments, your work goes beyond mere happenstance and into the intentional.

Moonstone
This semiprecious stone can be used by itself, or it can be worn in some type of setting (e.g. as a silver pendant or ring). The bluish white color has a multicolored luminescent quality that is especially apparent in natural light. In addition to its obvious beauty, moonstones are a powerful tool for two reasons:

> **Protection**
> It is the stone of Shekinah. Its feminine energy is symbolic *of* and draws Shekinah *to* it. It can help the practitioner focus on the Divine Presence in the midst of the demonic.
>
> **Prophecy**
> It can be a catalyst for prophetic abilities. When worn in earrings, one can receive auditory messages from Spirit. A pendant worn over the heart chakra, can open one to Divine love and supernatural insight. When placed under the tongue, it is thought to give one the ability to prophesy—especially during the waxing of the moon.

If you choose to try placing a moonstone on your tongue, it is **highly recommended that you use a moonstone pendant on a chain to prevent choking or swallowing.** This practice can be very dangerous, and the reader assumes all responsibility for his or her actions.

(Re)Considering Dreams

When my nephew Aidan was only a few months old, he started stiffening up and clenching one of his hands for no apparent reason. We soon found out these were seizures. Epilepsy doesn't run in our bloodline or in my sister-in-law's, and the doctors didn't really understand why he was having these sudden attacks. Everyone was desperate—petrified this was an indication of a serious condition.

A few nights after one of his longest episodes, my mother had a dream in which Aidan was able to speak; he told her to change his baby formula. Understandably, my mother didn't announce her revelation; she even thought it might only be her subconscious mind's way of dealing with the situation. Despite her hesitation, she decided to mention it to the doctor in a subtle but concerned manner. She said, "Could his formula have something to do with this?" It wasn't common for baby formula to provide such a violent negative reaction in newborns, so the doctor hadn't considered this possibility until she asked about it. A review of Aidan's previous blood panel and a few tests later revealed high iron levels in his blood. The formula he was drinking was iron-heavy to the point of being toxic. Immediately, his formula was changed and he never exhibited any seizure-like symptoms again. Without getting into an extensive discussion of dream interpretation, there are a few things to be learned from this.

First, most dreams should be taken at face value. I frequently dream of flying through crowded streets, but I hardly think this means I have any hidden ability to take flight like Peter Pan over London. The function of dreams has been explained from many perspectives including a survival/evolutionary standpoint, numerous psychological theories (e.g. fulfillment of subconscious desires), and as a physiological "file dump" not unlike a computer's hard drive. All of these have value and are a reminder of how far we've come as a civilization by knowing to discern between a natural bodily function and a spiritual experience.

As in the story I just mentioned, my mother was cautious for this very reason. Only *you* can determine a dream's purpose given the complexity of your background, life circumstance (e.g. stress, depression, and nutritional considerations), personal set of symbols and associations, and the way you are wired. My mother learned from this experience that her dreams may have clairvoyant or prophetic implications. **Her** experience has taught her to trust this gift when it manifests in a way that is evident to her. She can determine if a dream is based on everyday psychological or physiological needs or if it's a message coming from a higher level.

In this same way, I find the most effective way to make any magico-religious decision is based on experience. Self-inquiry or meta-cognition[21] allows us to evaluate our habits and what really makes us tick. Ultimately, this leads to insight. Think of a ritual, magical practice, devotion to a particular saint or deity, or anything of which you are a bit doubtful. Maybe you've tried candle magic once or twice and you're not sure if it's something you want to pursue. You may be doubtful of its effectiveness or even feel like it isn't necessarily consistent with what you have found as "truth," but you feel compelled to engage this a bit more. That desire is an obvious indication that candle magic may be a much-needed component of your path or practice; however, experience (i.e. "looking deeply") and a revised understanding can help you better make this decision. Consider the following questions:

- What thoughts do I have about _____ right now? Why? Are my impressions peaceful,

---

[21] Meta-cognition is the very natural practice of becoming aware of the self. It's not a spiritual practice, per se; it's more of an awareness of our mental processes and thought patterns. We step outside of our own conditioning, biases, and preconceived notions to look at the world without assigning a value judgment. In Vietnamese Zen practice, Master Thich Nhat Hahn calls this "looking deeply."

anxious, or indifferent? How else might I classify my first response to this?
- What's behind this emotion? Is it a reflexive response based on inexperience or unfamiliarity?
- Is _____ in direct opposition to the values and beliefs taught by my parents, family, teachers, and community? Is this something I know for myself, or is it conditioned? In other words, was the decision made for me early in life?
- What possible biases do I have? How can I be more objective without clinging to my usual likes and dislikes?
- Is my experience limited to sensationalized exposure? Have I merely heard about this from a friend of a friend? This can lead to perceptions based on urban legends and exaggerated stories.
- Was a Hollywood film my first teacher in this case? If so, special effects, audience expectations, a mainstream point-of-view, and the drive to earn revenue may have provided a severely distorted experience.
- Am I afraid of how others may perceive me? Does this really matter? Why or why not?
- What can **I** do to ensure the final decision is based on **my direct experience** for **my** greatest good?

The Miraculous Medal

The act of wearing a religious medal is not an ancient practice. Of course, organic items like teeth, bones, wooden beads, and other talismans were used; however, they were not as stylized as the Miraculous Medal of the Blessed Virgin Mary.

The use of this charm only dates back a couple centuries. Before people were wearing St. Christopher or St. Anthony medals, the first of its kind of sacramental was created at the direction of the Holy Mother herself.

St. Catherine Laboure received a vision of the BVM in 1830 in which she saw the Queen of Heaven with showers of light raining from her hands onto the earth below. Surrounding her was the prayer, "O Mary, conceived without sin, pray for us who have recourse to thee." Almost like a hologram, the vision rotated to illustrate how the back should appear. It contained 12 stars (representing the 12 apostles and the 12 tribes of Israel), a monogram consisting of an "M" for Mary that was topped with a cross, and the Sacred Heart of Jesus and Miraculous Heart of Mary just below.

Since the production of the first round of medals in 1832, many have claimed miracles, healings, and other graces. Personal testimonies of these types of events led to a widespread devotion of wearing the medal and frequently reciting the prayer inscribed on the front. For this reason, the medal has become known as "miraculous."

The Exorcism Medal of St. Benedict

This sacramental is worn or used for the very purpose of protection from Satan and all things demonic, and it is also referred to as The Jubilee Medal of St. Benedict. Because of the power of this charm, it is often placed within the foundation of buildings before the cement dries, between mattresses and box springs, and attached to rosaries and other religious items.

As the patron of exorcists, St. Benedict's medal is especially apropos in all situations involving low spirits. In addition to bearing the image of Holy Father Benedict, there are myriad symbols, Latin phrases, and abbreviated invocations hidden within the design.

FRONT OF MEDAL—LATIN INSCRIPTIONS[22]

TOP: Pax, "Peace"

CIRCLED LETTERS: CSPB (**C**rux **S**ancti **P**ater **B**enedicti), "Cross of Holy Father Benedict"

VERTICAL BAR OF CROSS: CSSML (**C**rux **S**acra **S**it **M**ihi **L**ux), "May the Holy Cross be my light"

HORIZONTAL BAR OF CROSS: NDSMD (**N**on **D**raco **S**it **M**ihi **D**ux), "Let not the dragon be my guide"

AROUND EDGE—RIGHT: VRSNSMV (**V**ade **R**etro, **S**atana! **N**unquam **S**uade **M**ihi **V**ana.), "Begone, Satan! Suggest not vain things to me."

AROUND EDGE—LEFT: SMQLIVB (**S**unt **M**ala **Q**uae **L**ibas **I**pse **V**enena **B**ibas.), "Evil is the cup thou offerest; Drink thou thine own poison."

---

[22] St. Gregory the Great. (n.d.). *The Life of St. Benedict*. Available from http://olrl.org/sacramental/benedictmedal.shtml

EXORCIST RISING

BACK OF MEDAL—LATIN INSCRIPTIONS[23]

FLANKING ST. BENEDICT: Crux S. Patris Benedicti, "Cross of Holy Father Benedict"

AROUND EDGE: Eius in obitu nostro praesentia muniamur., "May his presence protect us in the hour of our death."

BOTTOM: Ex SM Casino MDCCCLXXX, "From holy Monte Cassino, 1880."

---

[23] Ibid.

Anointing Oils

Second only to candles, oils and fragrances are one of the most timeless tools of exorcism and other magico-religious work. In addition to having a pleasant fragrance, oils continue to be used for mystical purposes such as anointing the living and preparing the dead. Rather than investing a lot of time and money into several oils, it's best to begin with a few and see which render the best results. Here are a few things to keep in mind when working with oils:

- Keep them in a cool, dry place—preferably out of direct sunlight. I usually store mine in blue or amber glass bottles.
- Never use the concentrated version of an oil (usually termed "essential") without diluting it first. Many are flammable or too harsh for use on the skin.
- Dilute essential oils in a "carrier." Olive oil (extra virgin is best) or jojoba are the most commonly used. Mineral or baby oil are not recommended.
- "Blends" are much less expensive and have been pre-diluted. These are perfect for immediate use.
- When creating your own blend, use cassia, cinnamon, and allspice sparingly. These tend to overpower the subtlety of other fragrances.
- Never refrigerate oils. At best, they will begin to crystalize; at worst, they will become rancid.
- Use common sense, and always keep oils away from pets and children.

When anointing a person with oil, it is typically applied to the forehead in conjunction with chirothesy. Although there is no wrong way to do this, the typical custom is to apply the oil to your finger and apply it to the forehead in the shape of a ✛ (symbolic of a cross). Anointing candles (also called "fixing" or "preparing") for a ritual also includes applying it with your finger. The usual method for novena candles is to make a circular pattern on the exposed surface (clockwise to cause something; counterclockwise to undo or prevent something).

Choosing oils should be done by the leading of Spirit or through cleromancy. Regardless of how a merchant suggests an oil be used, always trust your inner voice. Be confident in the purpose that is right for you and your particular situation. There are several good books that go into great detail about properties and (suggested) uses available. In addition to your own experience, you may want to consult other print and electronic sources. The following list is a small sampling of what I use or have used with success. I make some of these on my own; others are purchased from a botanica or online merchant.

Allspice	Frankincense	Louisiana Van
Bend Over	Gardenia	Van
Cassia	High John the	Myrrh
Come to Me	Conqueror	Nag Champa
Crossing	Hyacinth	Patchouli
Crossroads	Hyssop	Run, Devil, Run
Double Cross	Lavender	Sandalwood
Flying Devil	Lemon Verbena	Tonka Bean

Green Scapular

Many Catholics do not consider this a true scapular—they see it as an object of superstition. Of those that believe in the power of this sacramental, it is an indication of one's devotion to the Immaculate Heart of Mary and her power to rescue its wearer from a "sudden and unprovided for death."

The basic belief is that devotees are blessed with special graces against demonic encounters and other life-threatening situations.

The scapular is a simple square of green fabric (usually 100% wool) with a durable cord for wearing it around the neck. One side features an image of the Queen of Heaven; the other bears her Immaculate Heart encircled by a simple prayer: "Immaculate Heart of Mary, pray for us now and at the hour of our death." This simple talisman represents the boldness of one's belief in the power of Shekinah and in this short invocation against the demonic. This is especially true in cases of entities causing self-destructive behaviors, alcoholism, and other addictions. Some place the scapular in the pillowcase of the afflicted rather than trying to persuade them to wear it.

The Language of Numbers
Speaking very generally, numerology typically falls into one of two extremes. The first of these is the almost incomprehensible process of sifting through charts of arcane symbols, fragments of ancient languages, and corresponding numerical values in an attempt to find some sort of correlation. I tip my proverbial hat to those with the patience and even slightest understanding of this type of work—it's an undertaking, indeed. At the same time, the point of this type of text or system is supposed to be difficult for the uninitiated to understand.

The other extreme can be found in numerology books found at new age or occult shops that basically tell you what a number represents with no explanation. The author assigns a list of related terms to the number, but he or she never tells us exactly why these relationships supposedly exist. Simply stated, it seems (and probably is) just random.

When working against the demonic, there are two numbers that I find particularly effective. Unlike the scenarios I've just presented, I'll keep it simple and tell you why these numbers have spiritual significance. When I say to "use a number," it can refer to a lot of different things. It could be the quantity of candles you include when setting the lights, the number of times you anoint a person or home with oil, or the number of times you repeat a prayer. In addition to using the numbers suggested below, you may find others that are useful when working to expel dark entities.

The Power of 4

Four is like the smart bomb of numbers. It is the number of perfection and balance. Specifically, it represents the four corners of the cross, which is obvious in its symbolism, and it is also reflective of the crossroads of St. Lazarus in the New Orleanian tradition (i.e. the intersection of the natural and the supernatural—the gateway of the spirit world).

Most importantly, it is indicative of the Blood of Christ, which is the consummate remedy of any demonic attack, confrontation, or infestation. The restorative power of the Blood of Christ is revealed in the fourfold words of the Prophet Isaiah—specifically, in the following four stanzas of the 53rd chapter:

> [1] *But he was wounded for our transgressions,*
> [2] *he was bruised for our iniquities:*
> [3] *the chastisement of our peace was upon him;*
> [4] *and with his stripes we are healed.* (v. 5, KJV)

The Power of 9

Nine is the number of Shekinah, empowerment, fulfillment, and spiritual authority. The roots of this significance lie within the New Testament, Catholicism, and Magico-Religious tradition. After his resurrection, Jesus promised his Blessed Mother, disciples, and followers authority over the demonic by virtue of the Holy Ghost (i.e. the indwelling of Shekinah): "For John truly baptized with water; but ye shall be baptized with the Holy Ghost not many days hence."[24] Nine days passed between Christ's ascension into Heaven, and the descent of Shekinah onto the faithful.

---

[24] Acts 1:5 (KJV)

This nine day waiting period was taken very literally by Catholics and practitioners alike. It became the mystical number of prayers known as "novenas." When praying for a particular intention, a saint (one's patron or one specific to the need) is petitioned for nine days. Either using a "traditional" prayer to the saint or a specific novena prayer, the supplicant recites the prayer nine times in a row for a period of nine days. For some, the final requirement for holding a novena is to pass the prayer and story of fulfillment to nine other people. This is an act of thankfulness and praise to the intercessory power of the saint.

The most common novena is said to St. Jude and is "never known to fail." St. Jude is the patron of last resort and hopeless causes, and he welcomes any and all petitions (demonically-related or otherwise). For readers compelled to try this practice, I offer the following prayer. I also recommend *Novena: The Power of Prayer* (ISBN 0-670-88444-8),[25] as an additional resource of novenas for nearly every predicament or hardship.

Novena Prayer to St. Jude
Most holy St. Jude, faithful servant and friend of Jesus you are the patron of difficult cases. Pray for me, I am so helpless and alone. Intercede with God for me that He bring visible and speedy help where help is almost despaired of.

Come to my assistance in this great need that I may receive the consolation and help of heaven in all my necessities, tribulations, and sufferings, particularly **[mention your request here]** *and that I may praise God with you and all the saints forever. I promise, O Blessed St. Jude, to be ever mindful of this great favor granted me by God and to always honor you as my special and*

---

[25] Calamari, B. & DiPasqua, S. (1999). *Novena: The power of prayer.* New York: Penguin Putman, Inc.

powerful patron, and to gratefully encourage devotion to you.

Amen.

Other Examples of Mystical Numbers
7 Healing, cleansing, cures:
Based on the biblical account of Naaman being cured of leprosy after dipping himself in the Jordan River seven times (see 2 Kings 5)

Supernatural victory, claiming your birthright:
Based on the use of seven during the siege of the City of Jericho (see Joshua 6)

12 Protection of home, family, and property:
Based on the number of the tribes of Israel, the number of gems worn by Aaron and other Levite priests, the number of Christ's apostles, the number of stars crowning the Queen of Heaven in The Apocalypse/Revelation (see Revelation 12)

28 Divine courage, restraint:
Based on the number of stairs Christ climbed to receive his death sentence at the throne of Pontius Pilate.

33 Spiritual authority, supernatural abilities:
Based on the lifespan of Jesus.

Murray and Lanman Florida Water® (Cologne)[26]

This fresh, citrusy fragrance is applied by spraying it in a fine mist or by sprinkling. In magico-religious and New Orleanian circles, it is applied to individuals, ritual objects, on doorposts, and throughout homes. Florida Water is believed to prevent negative/demonic attacks, and practitioners use it as a tonic of anointing, protection, healing, and cleansing. I personally keep Florida Water on hand at all times because of its versatility.

While the manufacturers make no claims to any curative or supernatural efficacy of the product, many people buy it for these very reasons. I've encountered a few folks that attempt to create their own version of the powerful cologne, but I don't recommend it. Authentic Florida Water has been available for purchase in the U.S. for over 200 years. Why tamper with perfection?

Many botanicas, occult shops, and new age stores carry Florida Water; I've also seen it sold in drugstores in Chicago, New Orleans, and Miami. For most readers, the easiest way to obtain this product is through an online distributor.

The Bottomless Curio Cabinet

Do tools really matter? Short answer: Not so much. I could write volumes about religious and metaphysical tools, props, and curiosities. I could continue with descriptions of Catholic rosaries and chaplets, Buddhist malas and prayer wheels, Hindu yantras and sacred mudras, and other objects like libation bottles, spirit trumpets, black mirrors—it's endless. I have devoted the last several decades to collecting, testing, and admiring curios of every kind, and a book about this may be forthcoming. For the purposes of exorcism and working against the demonic, the best tools aren't something that can be touched with our physical hands.

Your sincerity, passion, intention, and innate divinity are

---

[26] Murray & Lanman Florida Water is trademarked and patented by Lanman & Kemp-Barclay & Co., Inc. of New Jersey. The author does not speak on behalf of the owner/manufacturer.

what manifest the very thing you seek. The tools are there to place us in the appropriate mindset. We learn to associate certain smells with Spirit; we may learn that a particular Psalm is effective in times of dire need. Ultimately, everything in existence is imbued with the same cosmic essence. We are the ones that grant power. We are the ones that call on primal forces just waiting to be released for our greatest good—everything else is foreplay.

A common misconception with exorcism or any rite of magico-religious practice is that tools and accoutrements create the desired intention. Although well-meaning, some confuse authentic experience—that is, real power and undeniable results—for imitation. They mistake a ritual for a recipe; it is not like making a batch of banana nut bread or corn muffins. I can give you an exhaustive list of supplies that have worked for me, and tell you the outcome that I have achieved; however, most attempts to replicate that instance will be nothing more than a reenactment of something sacred to me.

Every object or ingredient carries a metaphysical essence or energy with it, and we need to take into account things like its origin. Was it a gift? Did you purchase the item? Is it something you made over a series of days or weeks? Once it is in your possession, you also need to consider its placement and storage. Is it nothing more than a knickknack or curio for ornamental purposes? Is it brought out only when used? Is it maintained, kept clean, and treated with the appropriate level of respect? Carefully consider your tools.

Coupled with intention, our results are based on the totality of our practice. If you want to catch a wild boar, you have to know its temperament, respect its habitat, and take great care in approaching the venture. Rushing into any type of preternatural situation can be deadly at worst and futile at best.

Here's the good news: The fact that you are taking the time to read this book illustrates a level of commitment that is indicative of the type of practitioner and exorcist you will be. You're serious about knowing the nature of the demonic, operating within the power of Shekinah, and deepening your life at a fundamental level. No ordination is needed, and spectators just become a distraction. With the right intention, humility, and respect for the unseen forces occupying the same space as us, you *will know* when you're adequately prepared. There will be no need to look any further, to join the latest spiritual fad, or to question the authenticity of your experience again. Like the transfigured Christ or Rumi dancing in his own blood, your experience will speak for itself.

Invoking the Saints

Saint veneration is a significant part of magico-religious practice. While mainstream religion may recognize and honor a few saints, they do so with significant reservation. There is a fear of "idolatry," placing more emphasis on celestial helpers than God, and other similar types of nonsense that limits the rich experience offered in the company of this "great cloud of witnesses." I've been witness *to* and recipient *of* the power of these peculiar figures. While entire volumes have been written about the lives of saints of all faiths, I have included a select few for your consideration.

I could devote an entire book to my experiences, but our focus is exorcism and demonology. For this reason, I've chosen a sampling to help the aspiring practitioner get a sense of those that I've found helpful in dealing with low spirits and dark entities, but I strongly encourage further exploration. The saints to which I'm drawn may or may not be appealing to all readers, and there is no shortage of others from which to choose. The importance of "the communion of saints" referenced in The Apostle's Creed is paramount. It is essential to the magico-religious life. Their patience is endless; their assistance is swift; and their love is unconditional.

NOAH TYSICK

St. Lazarus: Gatekeeper and Healer

All magico-religious practice begins at the crossroads. Knowledge and experience intersect at a point we call our "truth." While this truth is very personal, it is no more or less authentic than that of others.

There is a man at the crossroads. Some call him Legba, Papa Legba, or St. Peter. The most notable of his manifestations is St. Lazarus. Regardless of name, his appearance is deceptively meek—almost frail, but his authority cannot be overstated. He is the gatekeeper between the spirit world and the physical plane. Mortal and immortal alike are subject to his authority. When invoked, St. Lazarus controls the flow between worlds. He protects, prevents, and permits.

All practitioners should have some level of devotion to

St. Lazarus. In addition to his custodial role between spirit and matter, he is depicted in his sickly state (i.e. as a leper) prior to being healed by St. Peter. He is the great deliverer from demonic **oppression**, and he should be honored on one's altar in the form of a statue, holy card or print of some kind. His image or statue should be draped in a deep purple cloak or shawl in honor of his suffering and his spiritual majesty.

Invoked For
Assistance while working within spiritual realms. As the gatekeeper between the gross/physical and the subtle/supernatural, St. Lazarus manages the flow of energy passing between the various planes of existence.

Symbols and Colors[27]
Crutches, Green Maltese Cross, Three Shiny Pennies, (Coupling of) Red and Black, and Purple.

Gifts to the World
The Crossroads

The Crossroads
While most spiritual work should be performed at your home altar, there is an additional location used to meet with this saint. You can go to a literal crossroads just before sunrise with your request for assistance. It should be a safe location with no traffic and sufficient lighting:

1. State your specific petition as you approach the intersection.
2. When finished, it is customary to turn your back to the intersection.
3. Toss three shiny pennies over your left shoulder and say the following aloud three times:

Holy St. Lazarus, ora pro nobis!

---

[27] Colors associated with saints indicated which color candle may be used in conjunction with prayers, novenas, invocations, etc.

4. Cross yourself (i.e. do the sign of the cross) and quietly whisper the traditional Glory Be:

   Glory be to the Father, and to the Son, and to the Holy Spirit as it was in the beginning, is now, and ever shall be. World without end. Amen.

5. Walk away from the crossroads **without looking back**.

Prayer to St. Lazarus[28]

Dear patron and assistant of the poor and sick. With this prayer I request your assistance, and with the aid of the Holy Spirit may the Lord always protect me during sickness or in health Saint Lazarus give me the strength to overcome all the temptations on earth. In the name of the Father, the Son, and the Holy Spirit. Amen.

---

[28] All prayers in this section are traditional; however, practitioners often choose to address saints in a more conversational way.

St. Philomena: "Powerful with God"

St. Philomena is one of the gentlest yet most powerful saints. Little is known about her life, and her status as a "saint" by the Catholic Church is even in question despite her massive following. While the veneration of St. Philomena is not prohibited, it is not endorsed either. She is a sort of renegade saint in that her remains (skeletal and a vial of dried blood) are enshrined in the Church of Mungano in Italy (near Naples) in the grand style of a fully beatified and sainted individual.[29] Despite the lack of approval or endorsement, her cult status and powerful assistance endure.

---

[29] Kirsch, J.P. (1911). St. Philomena. In The Catholic Encyclopedia. New York: Robert Appleton Company. Retrieved from New Advent: http://www.new advent .org /cathen/12025b.htm

Invoked for
Demonic attacks against children, the elderly, and the helpless. With her support, we can discern hidden or underlying demonic activity and influence.

Symbols and Colors
Anchor, Arrow, Lilies, Palm Leaves, Pink, Green

Gifts to the World
Supernatural Knocking, Cord of St. Philomena

The Knocking Saint
She makes her presence known using three of something. Many have claimed to hear three knocks or raps when invoking her name or when a prayer has been answered. Confirmation of her power can also take the form of three consecutive flashes of household lights, ringing of a (door) bell, or other similar sign.

Cord of St. Philomena
This sacramental is made of red and white fibers braided in a way that shows an equal part of red (symbolic of her innocent blood) and white (representing her innocence). These are available at religious stores and are typically worn at the waist. I recommend cutting it into small segments (wrist and ankle bracelets or one-inch pieces) to be used/worn by the practitioner and the afflicted.

Prayer to St. Philomena
O St. Philomena, glorious Martyr of Faith and Purity, grant me the same strength of mind that enabled you to resist the most terrible assaults; grant me your ardent love for Jesus Christ which the most atrocious tortures were not able to extinguish, so that, by wearing your Cord and imitating you on earth, I will be coronated with you in heaven. Amen.

St. Michael the Archangel

He is the saint most invoked in national and international turmoil. Although many associate him with large-scale undertakings like preventing world war and genocide, he is not too big to help individuals. St. Michael is traditionally the patron of the military and law enforcement professionals, but I can attest to his personal intercessory power. He was the first saint I ever venerated, and I still recite his prayer on a regular basis.

Symbols and Colors
Shield, Sword or Spear, Serpents, Dragon, Green, and Red

Gifts to the World
Chaplet of St. Michael, Protection From Evil—Especially Against Satan Himself

Prayer to St. Michael
Saint Michael the Archangel, defend us in battle, be our protection against the wickedness and snares of the Devil. May God rebuke him, we humbly pray and do thou, O Prince of the Heavenly Host, by the Power of God, cast into Hell Satan and all the evil spirits who wander the world seeking the ruin of souls. Amen. ✜

St. Benedict

He is the patron of exorcists. St. Benedict wrote the initial rule for Western monasticism, which established how cloistered monks should structure their daily lives and behavior. More importantly, his devotion to the Holy Cross is unrivaled. Before eating, he always prayed and did the sign of the cross over his food. According to legend, an enemy tried to poison his wine, but the cup burst under Benedict's blessing. His life was saved—his supernatural gifts confirmed.

Symbols and Colors
Serpent, Chalice, Exorcism Medal of St. Benedict, The Crucifix of St. Benedict, Brown, Gold

Gifts to the World
The Jubilee Medal
The Benedictine Rule

Prayer to St. Benedict
O glorious St. Benedict, sublime model of all virtues, pure vessel of God's grace! Behold me, humbly kneeling at thy feet. I implore thy loving heart to pray for me before the throne of God. To thee I have recourse in all the dangers which daily surround me. Shield me against my enemies, inspire me to imitate thee in all things. May thy blessing be with me always, so that I may shun whatever God forbids and avoid the occasions of sin.

Graciously obtain for me from God those favors and graces of which I stand so much in need, in the trials, miseries and afflictions of life. Thy heart was always so full of love, compassion, and mercy towards those who were afflicted or troubled in any way. Thou didst never dismiss without consolation and assistance any one who had re-course to thee. I therefore invoke thy powerful intercession, in the confident hope that thou wilt hear my prayers and obtain for me the special grace and favor I so earnestly implore (mention it), if it be for the greater glory of God and the welfare of my soul.

Help me, O great St. Benedict, to live and die as a faithful child of God, to be ever submissive to His holy will, and to attain the eternal happiness of heaven. Amen.

St. Martin de Porres

St. Martin is one of the few documented saints of color. Although he is venerated within the Catholic Church, his true devotees are typically not taken to organized religion. In the (New) Orleanian sense, he is an agent for the Practice. His statues are often seen near doorways and on front porches as a marker that one is of a more magical (rather than of a religious) temperament. Unofficially, he is the patron of solitary practitioners.

Symbols and Colors
Broom, Tourniquet, Gold, Tan, Purple

Gifts to the World
Protection from Demonically Influenced/ Motivated People and Hatred Without a Cause

Prayer to St. Martin
To you Saint Martin de Porres, we prayerfully lift up our hearts filled with serene confidence and devotion. Mindful of your unbounded and helpful charity to all levels of society and also of your meekness and humility of heart, we offer our petitions to you. Pour out upon our families the precious gifts of your solicitous and generous intercession; show to the people of every race and every color the paths of unity and of justice; implore from our Father in heaven, so that through mutual benevolence in God we may increase in grace and merit the rewards of eternal life. Amen

Our Lady of Guadalupe

In Mexico City, there is a church that houses the Marian equivalent of the Shroud of Turin. When she appeared to Juan Diego in the 16th Century, she left a physical imprint or portrait of herself on his cloak (tilma). This full color, heavenly image is venerated by millions each year. Despite its age and the laws of nature, the cloth remains remarkably new in appearance and condition. Our Lady of Guadalupe is the Divine Mother in her most merciful form. She heals and protects against hate crimes and self-destruction (especially alcoholism).

Symbols and Colors
12 Stars, Sun, Moon, Roses, Pink, White, Green

Gifts to the World
Shekinah Embodied

Prayer to Our Lady Of Guadalupe
Our Lady of Guadalupe, Mystical Rose,
make intercession for holy Church,
protect the sovereign Pontiff,
help all those who invoke you in their necessities,
and since you are the ever Virgin Mary
and Mother of the true God,

obtain for us from your most holy Son
the grace of keeping our faith,
of sweet hope in the midst of the bitterness of life
of burning charity, and the precious gift
of final perseverance. Amen.

St. Joan of Arc

St. Joan of Arc is as well-known as a heroic figure as she is as a saint. Her fame is both regional and religious. As the Maid of Orleans, she is revered in New Orleans with near demigod status. In addition to her public monument on Decatur Street in the French Quarter, a near life-sized statue of her holds vigil at the back of St. Louis Cathedral in the Crescent City. Her bravery, spiritual discernment, and visions of St. Michael add to the Saint's supernatural appeal of exorcists.

Symbols and Colors
Fleur-de-lis, Sword, Red, White

Gifts to the World
Holy Rebellion, Supernatural Bravery

Prayer to St. Joan of Arc
O Joan, holy liberator of France, the powerful holy force in the days of old, as you yourself said, "Peace would be found only at the point of a lance," who used the weapons of war when no other means were able to obtain a just Peace, take care and help today those who do not want to do violence and patiently try to employ all possible peaceful means of resolution, but now allow the violence of war.

Return, O great hearted Daughter of God, and wage war against the enemies of the people of France and the people of England, with whom you yourself wished an alliance for the good of humanity. Both nations are now raised for the defense of what you would have defended: Justice between nations! Both peoples wish to crush the rebirth of barbarism as they raise this cry which is yours: Christianity must continue!

Heroine of Orleans, transmit to our leaders, your talent to inspire your soldiers to accomplish great deeds of valor, in order that our soldiers' efforts will come to a rapid and successful end.

Triumphant One of Reims, prepare for us the just peace under the shield of a force that will be henceforth vigilant!

Martyr of Rouen, be near to all the soldiers who fall in battle, in order to support, console, and help them and those dear ones that they leave behind.

Saint of the Country, excite in all souls, in every home of the world, the zeal to contribute to the salvation of the world and the return of peace, works which you crave, the rediscovery of a more Christian life, through holy thoughts and actions, forgiveness and persistent prayer, that as you yourself once said, "God must be served first." Amen.

St. Patrick

Contrary to popular belief, St. Patrick is not just the patron of Ireland. His magico-religious roots run deeply because of his association with serpents and snake imagery in general. According to legend, he drove all snakes (and "paganism') out of Ireland, but Practitioners understand the much richer implications of invoking his name. In addition to writing several prayers during his lifetime, his power over snakes (i.e. the demonic) is the greater ability. Although it can be difficult to extricate the historical from the folklore, the results of seeking his intercession are self-evident.

Symbols and Colors
Shamrock, Serpent, Shepherd's Staff, Green, White, Yellow

Gifts to the World
The Lorica or "Breastplate" Prayer

St. Patrick's Lorica (Excerpt)
Against all Satan's spells and wiles,
Against false words of heresy,
Against the knowledge that defiles,
Against the heart's idolatry,
Against the wizard's evil craft,
Against the death wound and the burning,
The choking wave and the poisoned shaft,
Protect me, Christ, 'til Thy returning.

Christ be with me, Christ within me,
Christ behind me, Christ before me,
Christ beside me, Christ to win me,
Christ to comfort and restore me.

Christ beneath me, Christ above me,
Christ in quiet, Christ in danger,
Christ in hearts of all that love me,
Christ in mouth of friend and stranger.

St. Expedite

St. Expedite is a bit controversial as far as the Catholic Church is concerned. While he is not an "official" saint, he is considered a martyr. Regardless of ecclesiastical approval (or lack thereof), the cult of St. Expedite is significant. It's not uncommon to see personal ads for favors granted in electronic and print sources. In magico-religious circles, he is usually invoked for financial and legal matters, but his all powerful intercession is especially effective in situations involving the demonic. While I have listed a prayer to him below, it is not uncommon for people to invoke him in a more conversational way.

Symbols and Colors
Cross, Palm Leaf, Shipping Crate, White, Green

Gifts to the World
Swift Intercession

Prayer to St. Expedite

*Our dear martyr and protector, Saint Expedite, You who know what is necessary and what is urgently needed. I beg you to intercede before the Holy Trinity, that by your grace my request will be granted **[Mention your request here]**. May I receive your blessings and favors. In the name of our Lord Jesus Christ, Amen.*

6 TRADITIONAL PRAYERS

*I would go to the deeps a hundred times to cheer a downcast spirit.
It is good for me to have been afflicted, that I might know how to
speak a word in season to one that is weary.*

~Charles Spurgeon

How to Use this Section
The following pages contain a collection of prayers I've used with success. They are arranged in no particular order, but I encourage the reader to peruse this section, mark selections that resonate, and follow the guidance of Shekinah when using them to assist those that are oppressed by demons and other low spirits. Casting the cowries or another form of cleromancy can be used to determine when and if to use any of these.

In some cases, the Latin and English versions have been included. If you use the Latin version, don't be overly concerned about exact pronunciation—Spirit knows what you're saying. Also note, there is a time for spontaneous prayer and chanting, and there are times in which century's old prayers may be more effectual. Each situation is as unique as the practitioner's selection or omission of prayer.

Finally, please note: When this symbol appears ✚, it is an indication that one should cross themselves and/or make the sign of the cross over the person or object at which the words are directed.

Signum Crucis
In nomine Patris, ✚ et Filii, et Spiritus Sancti. Amen.

Sign of the Cross
In the name of the Father, ✚ and of the Son, and of the Holy Ghost. Amen.

Oratio Dominica
Pater noster, qui es in caelis, sanctificetur nomen tuum. Adveniat regnum tuum. Fiat voluntas tua, sicut in caelo et in terra. Panem nostrum quotidianum da nobis hodie, et dimitte nobis debita nostra sicut et nos dimittimus debitoribus nostris. Et ne nos inducas in tentationem, sed libera nos a malo. Amen.

The Lord's Prayer
Our Father, Who art in heaven, Hallowed be Thy Name. Thy Kingdom come. Thy Will be done, on earth as it is in Heaven. Give us this day our daily bread. And forgive us our trespasses, as we forgive those who trespass against us. And lead us not into temptation, but deliver us from evil. Amen.

Ave Maria
Ave Maria, gratia plena, Dominus tecum. Benedicta tu in mulieribus, et benedictus fructus ventris tui, Iesus. Sancta Maria, Mater Dei, ora pro nobis peccatoribus, nunc, et in hora mortis nostrae. Amen.

Hail Mary
Hail Mary, full of grace, The Lord is with thee. Blessed art thou among women, and blessed is the fruit of thy womb, Jesus. Holy Mary, Mother of God, pray for us sinners now, and at the hour of death. Amen.

Doxologia Minor (Gloria)
Gloria Patri, et Filio, et Spiritui Sancto. Sicut erat in principio, et nunc, et semper, et in saecula saeculorum. Amen.

Minor Doxology (Glory Be)
Glory be to the Father, and to the Son, and to the Holy Spirit. As it was in the beginning, is now, and ever shall be, world without end. Amen.

Salve Regina
Salve Regina, Mater misericordiae. Vita, dulcedo, et spes nostra, salve. Ad te clamamus exsules filii Hevae. Ad te Suspiramus, gementes et flentes in hac lacrimarum valle. Eia ergo, Advocata nostra, illos tuos misericordes oculos ad nos converte. Et Iesum, benedictum fructum ventris tui, nobis post hoc exsilium ostende. O clemens, o pia, o dulcis Virgo Maria. Ora pro nobis, Sancta Dei Genetrix.
Ut digni efficiamur promissionibus Christi.

Hail, Holy Queen
Hail, holy Queen, mother of mercy, our life, our sweetness, and our hope. To thee do we cry, poor banished children of Eve. To thee do we send up our sighs mourning and weeping in this valley of tears. Turn then, most gracious advocate, thine eyes of mercy toward us, and after this our exile show us the blessed fruit of thy womb, Jesus. O clement, O loving, O sweet Virgin Mary. Pray for us, O Holy Mother of God. That we may be made worthy of the promises of Christ.

Symboloum Apostolorum

Credo in Deum Patrem omnipotentem, Creatorem caeli et terrae; et in Jesum Christum, Filium eius unicum, Dominum nostrum; qui conceptus est de Spiritu Sancto, natus ex Maria Virgine; passus sub Pontio Pilato, crucifixus, mortuus, et sepultus; descendit ad inferos; tertia die resurrexit a mortuis; ascendit ad caelos, sedet ad dexteram Dei Patris omnipotentis; inde venturus est judicare vivos et mortuos.

Credo in Spiritum Sanctum; sanctam Ecclesiam catholicam, sanctorum communionem; remissionem peccatorum; carnis resurrectionem; vitam aeternam.

Amen. ✚

The Apostles Creed

I believe in God, the Father Almighty, Creator of Heaven and earth; and in Jesus Christ, His only Son Our Lord, Who was conceived by the Holy Spirit, born of the Virgin Mary, suffered under Pontius Pilate, was crucified, died, and was buried. He descended into Hell; the third day He rose again from the dead; He ascended into Heaven, and sitteth at the right hand of God, the Father almighty; from whence He shall come to judge the living and the dead.

I believe in the Holy Spirit, the holy Catholic Church, the communion of saints, the forgiveness of sins, the resurrection of the body and life everlasting.

Amen. ✚

EXORCIST RISING

Libera Me

The following is actually sung during the Requiem Mass or Mass for the Dead. Because of the centuries of repetition and usage, recitation of it is particularly potent. While it may seem a bit apocalyptic at first glance, it speaks to the ultimate authority of Shekinah (i.e. holy "fire") against the demonic. I strongly recommend the frequent and fervent use of this prayer in Latin.

Latin
Libera me, Domine, de morte aeterna in die illa tremenda quando coeli movendi sunt et terra, dum veneris judicare saeculum per ignem.

Tremens factus sum ego et timeo, dum discussion venerit atque venture ira: quando coeli movendi sunt et terra.

English
Deliver me, O Lord, from eternal death on that awful day when the heavens and earth shall be shaken and you shall come to judge the world by fire.

I am seized with fear and trembling by the trial at hand and the wrath that is to come: when the heavens and earth shall be shaken.

NOAH TYSICK

The Confiteor

*Traditionally, this is a prayer used during some Catholic Masses as a form of public confession of "sin." Regardless of your personal beliefs regarding the notions of sin and reconciliation, the benefits of using this prayer as preparation for any magico-religious work cannot be overstated. As with **Libera Me**, the Latin version is the most powerful. It speaks to the supplicant at a cellular level that has to be experienced to understand.*

Confiteor Deo omnipotenti, beatae Mariae semper Virgini, beato Michaeli Archangelo, beato Joanni Baptistae, sanctis Apostolis Petro et Paulo, omnibus Sanctis, et vobis, fratres (et tibi Pater), quia peccavi nimis cogitatione, verbo et opere: mea culpa, mea culpa, mea maxima culpa. Ideo precor beatam Mariam semper Virginem, beatum Michaelem Archangelum, beatum, Joannem Baptistam, sanctos Apostolos Petrum et Paulum, omnes Sanctos et te, Pater, orare pro me ad Dominum Deum nostrum.

I confess to Almighty God, to blessed Mary ever Virgin, to blessed Michael, the Archangel, to blessed John the Baptist, to the holy Apostles Peter and Paul, to all the Saints and to you, Father, that I have sinned exceedingly, in thought, word and deed, through my fault, through my fault, through my most grievous fault. Therefore I beseech the blessed Mary, ever Virgin, blessed Michael the Archangel, blessed John the Baptist, the holy Apostles Peter and Paul, all the Saints, and you, Father, to pray to the Lord our God for me.

EXORCIST RISING

Magnificat[30]

This is the only prayer spoken by the Blessed Virgin Mary on record. It is not a prayer in the sense that she is asking for something; rather, her words are an ecstatic exclamation of thanksgiving. Practitioners may find this as a useful tool to (like the Blessed Mother) invoke Shekinah.

Magnificat anima mea Dominum: et exsultavit spiritus meus in Deo, salutari meo. Quia respexit humilitatem ancillae suae: ecce enim ex hoc beatam me dicent omnes generationes. Quia fecit mihi magna qui potens est: et sanctum nomen eius. Et misericordia eius a progenie in progenies timentibus eum. Fecit potentiam in bracchio suo: dispersit superbos mente cordis sui. Deposuit potentes de sede, et exaltavit humiles. Esurientes implevit bonis: et divites dimisit inanes. Suscepit Israel, puerum suum,	My soul doth magnify the Lord, And my spirit hath rejoiced in God my Saviour. For he hath regarded the low estate of his handmaiden: for, behold, from henceforth all generations shall call me blessed. For he that is mighty hath done to me great things; and holy is his name. And his mercy is on them that fear him from generation to generation. He hath shewed strength with his arm; he hath scattered the proud in the imagination of their hearts. He hath put down the mighty from their seats, and exalted them of low

---

[30] To be followed by the Minor Doxology ("Gloria" or "Glory Be").

NOAH TYSICK

recordatus misericordiae suae. Sicut locuts est ad patres nostros, Abraham et semini eius in saecula.

degree. He hath filled the hungry with good things; and the rich he hath sent empty away. He hath helped his servant Israel, in remembrance of his mercy; As He spake to our fathers, to Abraham, and to His seed forever.

The Memorare

Memorare literally translates to "remember." It is in this ancient prayer that one can invoke the powerful intercession of the Blessed Virgin Mary, Queen of Heaven, Shekinah, etc. This invocation is particularly interesting because of the mystique surrounding its author. Some have speculated Egyptian origins as old as 2000 BC, and others have credited it to various Catholic Saints including St. Augustine (354-430 AD) and St. Bernard (1090-1153).[31] Memorization of this prayer is highly recommended.

Remember, O most gracious Virgin Mary, that never was it known that anyone who fled to thy protection, implored thy help, or sought thine intercession was left unaided. Inspired by this confidence, I fly unto thee, O Virgin of virgins, my mother; to thee do I come, before thee I stand, sinful and sorrowful. O Mother of the Word Incarnate, despise not my petitions, but in thy mercy hear and answer me.

---

[31] Bazzett, M. (2012). Holy Mary, pray for us. *CatholicCulture.org*. Retrieved from http://www.catholicculture.org/culture/library/view.cfm?recnum=984

NOAH TYSICK

Litany of the Blessed Virgin Mary

A litany is a prayer that takes on a chant-like quality. The repetition of phrases can be effective as part of one's daily practice or as a preparatory tool in anticipation of meeting with those that may be afflicted. Traditionally, at least two people are needed (one to say the first line and another to utter the response), but it is just as effective when said privately or without a respondent. The Litany of the Blessed Virgin Mary is one of the most commonly used.

Lord, have mercy on us.
—Christ, have mercy on us.
Lord, have mercy on us.
Christ, hear us.
—Christ, graciously hear us.
God the Father of Heaven,
—Have mercy on us.
God the Son, Redeemer of the world,
—Have mercy on us.
God the Holy Ghost,
—Have mercy on us.
Holy Trinity, one God,
—Have mercy on us.

Holy Mary—pray for us.
Holy Mother of God—pray for us.
Holy Virgin of virgins—pray for us.
Mother of Christ—pray for us.
Mother of divine grace—pray for us.
Mother most pure—pray for us.
Mother most chaste—pray for us.
Mother inviolate—pray for us.
Mother undefiled—pray for us.
Mother most amiable—pray for us.
Mother most admirable—pray for us.
Mother of good counsel—pray for us.
Mother of our Creator—pray for us.

Mother of our Savior—pray for us.
Virgin most prudent—pray for us.
Virgin most venerable—pray for us.
Virgin most renowned—pray for us.
Virgin most powerful—pray for us.
Virgin most merciful—pray for us.
Virgin most faithful—pray for us.
Mirror of justice—pray for us.
Seat of wisdom—pray for us.
Cause of our joy—pray for us.
Spiritual vessel—pray for us.
Vessel of honor—pray for us.
Singular vessel of devotion—pray for us.
Mystical rose—pray for us.
Tower of David—pray for us.
Tower of ivory—pray for us.
House of gold—pray for us.
Ark of the Covenant—pray for us.
Gate of Heaven—pray for us.
Morning star—pray for us.
Health of the sick—pray for us.
Refuge of sinners—pray for us.
Comforter of the afflicted—pray for us.
Help of Christians—pray for us.
Queen of angels—pray for us.
Queen of patriarchs—pray for us.
Queen of prophets—pray for us.
Queen of apostles—pray for us.
Queen of martyrs—pray for us.
Queen of confessors—pray for us.
Queen of innocence—pray for us.
Queen of all saints—pray for us.
Queen conceived without Original Sin—pray for us.
Queen assumed into Heaven—pray for us.
Queen of the most holy Rosary—pray for us.
Queen of peace—pray for us.

Lamb of God, who takes away the sins of the world—Spare us, O Lord.
Lamb of God, who takes away the sins of the world—Graciously hear us, O Lord.
Lamb of God, who takes away the sins of the world—Have mercy on us.

Pray for us, O Holy Mother of God—That we may be made worthy of the promises of Christ.

Litany of the Most Precious Blood of Jesus

The Blood of Christ is the greatest weapon for binding and driving out Satan and all demonic entities. Even for those that do not subscribe to orthodox Christianity, there is no greater invocation than "pleading The Blood." This may seem a bit brutal to our modern sensibilities, but I can personally attest to The Power of the Blood.

Lord, have mercy.
—Lord, have mercy.
Christ, have mercy.
—Christ, have mercy.
Lord, have mercy.
—Lord, have mercy.

Christ, hear us.
—Christ, hear us.
Christ, graciously hear us.
—Christ, graciously hear us.

God the Father of Heaven—have mercy on us.
God the Son, Redeemer of the world—have mercy on us.
God, the Holy Spirit—have mercy on us.
Holy Trinity, One God—have mercy on us.

Blood of Christ, only-begotten Son of the eternal Father,
—save us.
Blood of Christ, Incarnate Word or God,
—save us.
Blood of Christ, of the New and Eternal Testament,
—save us.
Blood of Christ, falling upon the earth in Agony,
—save us.
Blood of Christ, shed profusely in the Scourging,
—save us.
Blood of Christ, flowing forth in the Crowning with Thorns,

—save us.

Blood of Christ, poured out on the Cross,
—save us.
Blood of Christ, price of our salvation,
—save us.
Blood of Christ, without which there is no forgiveness,
—save us.
Blood of Christ, Eucharistic drink and refreshment of souls,
—save us.
Blood of Christ, stream of mercy,
—save us.
Blood of Christ, victor over demons,
—save us.
Blood of Christ, courage of Martyrs,
—save us.
Blood of Christ, strength of Confessors,
—save us.
Blood of Christ, bringing forth innocence,
—save us.
Blood of Christ, help of those in peril,
—save us.
Blood of Christ, relief of the burdened,
—save us.
Blood of Christ, solace in sorrow,
—save us.
Blood of Christ, hope of the penitent,
—save us.
Blood of Christ, consolation of the dying,
—save us.
Blood of Christ, peace and tenderness of hearts,
—save us.
Blood of Christ, pledge of eternal life,
—save us.
Blood of Christ, freeing souls from purgatory,
—save us.
Blood of Christ, most worthy of all glory and honor,

—save us.

Lamb of God, who taketh away the sins of the world,
—spare us, O Lord.
Lamb of God, who taketh away the sins of the world,
—graciously hear us, O Lord.
Lamb of God, who taketh away the sins of the world,
—have mercy on us, O Lord.

Exorcism Prayer of St. Michael the Archangel

This prayer should not be confused with The Roman Ritual or The Rite of Exorcism. It is critical to reiterate the importance of addressing the demonic spirit rather than the person. Practitioners may use this to bind and drive away demonic influences on people, places, and even objects.

✝ In the name of the Father, and of the Son, and of the Holy Ghost. Amen.[32]

Most glorious prince of the celestial host, Saint Michael the archangel, defend us in the conflict which we have to sustain against principalities and powers, against the rulers of the world of this darkness, against the spirits of wickedness in the high places.

---

[32] When ✝ appears, it is an indication that one should cross themselves and/or make the sign of the cross over the person or object at which the words are directed.

EXORCIST RISING

Come to the rescue of us whom God has created in His image and likeness, and whom He has redeemed at a great price from the tyranny of the Devil. It is thou whom we venerate as our guardian and protector; thou whom the Lord has charged to conduct redeemed souls into Heaven.

Pray, therefore, the God of Peace to subdue Satan beneath our feet, that he may no longer retain humanity captive. Present our prayers to the Most High, that without delay they may draw his mercy down upon us. Seize the dragon, the old serpent, which is the Devil and Satan, bind him and cast him into the bottomless pit, that he may no more deceive the nations.

In the name of Jesus Christ, our Lord and Savior, strengthened by the intercession of the Immaculate Virgin Mary, Mother of God, of blessed Michael the Archangel, of the blessed Apostles Peter and Paul, and all the Saints, we confidently undertake to repulse the attacks and deceits of the Devil. Amen. ✚

Let God arise, and let His enemies be scattered: and let them that hate Him flee from before His face. As smoke vanishes, so let them vanish away: as wax melts before the fire, so let the wicked perish at the presence of God.

v. Behold the Cross of the Lord! Flee, bands of enemies.
r. The Lion of the Tribe of Judah, the offspring of David, has prevailed.
v. May Thy mercy descend upon us.
r. As great as our hope in Thee.

We drive you from us, whoever you may be, unclean spirits, Satanic powers, deaf and dumb squatters, wicked legions, assemblies, and sects. In the Name and by the virtue of Our Lord Jesus Christ ✚.

May you be bound and driven away from this place and from the souls redeemed by the Precious Blood of the Divine Lamb ✚.

Cease by your audacity, cunning serpent, to deceive the human race, to persecute the church, to torment God's elect, and to sift them as wheat ✚. This is the command made to you by the Most High God ✚, with whom in your haughty insolence you still pretend to be equal ✚. The God who will save all humanity and bring them to the knowledge of the truth. God the Father commands you ✚. God the Son commands you ✚. God the Holy Ghost commands you ✚.

Jesus Christ, the Eternal Word of God Made Flesh, commands you ✚. He, who to save our race, outdone through your malice, humbled Himself, becoming obedient unto death. He who has built His Church on the firm rock and declared that the gates of Hell shall not prevail against her, because He dwells with her all days, even to the consummation of the world. The hidden virtue of the Cross requires it of you, as does the power of the mysteries of the Christian Faith ✚. The Glorious Mother of God, the Virgin Mary, commands you ✚. She, who by her humility and from the first moment of her Immaculate Conception, crushed your proud head. The faith of the Holy Apostles Peter and Paul and of the other Apostles commands you ✚.

The blood of the Martyrs and the pious intercession of all the Saints command you ✢.

Thus, cursed dragon, and you, wicked legions, we charge you by the Living God ✢, by the True God ✢, by the Holy God ✢, by the God who so loved the world, as to give up his only-begotten Son that whosoever believes in Him may not perish but may have life everlasting. Cease deceiving human creatures and pouring out to them the poison of eternal perdition. Cease harming the Church and hindering her liberty. Loose, Satan, inventor and master of all deceit, enemy of humanity's salvation.

Surrender the place to Jesus in whom you have found none of your works—the Lord rebuke you. Surrender the place to the one, holy, catholic, and Apostolic Church acquired by Jesus at the price of His Blood—the Lord rebuke you.

Stoop beneath **the all-powerful hand of God. Tremble and flee at the evocation of The Most Holy and Terrible Name of Jesus;** this Name which causes Hell to tremble; this Name to which the virtues, powers and dominations of Heaven are humbly submissive; this Name which the cherubim and seraphim praise unceasingly, repeating: "Holy, Holy, Holy is the Lord God of hosts. Heaven and earth are full of your glory."

v. O Lord hear my prayer.
r. And let my cry come unto Thee.
v. May the Lord be with thee.
r. And with thy spirit.

Let us pray. God of heaven, God of earth, God of angels, God of archangels, God of patriarchs, God of prophets, God of apostles, God of martyrs, God of confessors, God of the innocent, God who has power to give life after death and rest after work, because there is no other God than Thee and there can be no other, for Thou art the creator of all things, visible and invisible, of whose reign there shall be no end. We humbly prostrate ourselves before Thy glorious majesty, and we supplicate Thee to deliver us from all the tyranny of the low spirits, from their snares, their lies, and their furious wickedness. Deign, O Lord, to protect us by thy power and to preserve us safe and sound. We beseech thee through Jesus Christ Our Lord. Amen ✞.

v. From the snares of the Devil,
r. Deliver us, O Lord.
v. That we may have life—that we may live it abundantly in peace and liberty,
r. We beseech Thee to hear us.
v. That Thou would crush down all demonic enemies,
r. We beseech Thee to hear us.

(Holy water is sprinkled in or on the appropriate place.)

Saint Michael the Archangel, defend us in battle, be our protection against the wickedness and snares of the Devil. May God rebuke him, we humbly pray and do thou, O Prince of the Heavenly Host, by the Power of God, cast into Hell Satan and all the evil spirits who wander the world seeking the ruin of souls. Amen. ✞

7 MAGICO-RELIGIOUS PSALMS

Mysteries are feminine; they like to veil themselves
but still want to be seen and divined.

~Karl Wilhelm Friedrich Schlegel

The Power of Words
We have all been in a situation in which we found ourselves saying, "I realized it was true when I finally said it out loud." Common examples of this are usually traumatic experiences like the death of someone dear or the dissolution of a marriage. Words confirm reality, but that is not the end of the matter: Words also create reality. We shape our world, our perceptions, our lives by the things we utter. It is in our nature to create, and we can talk ourselves into having a good day or into coming down with the flu. We can tell ourselves how inadequate we are, and we will do everything to prove ourselves correct. When we say the words, "I love you," the utterance has a twofold benefit.

1. **It confirms our reality**:
    We know how we feel about a particular person

or potential partner. We have rehearsed scenarios of how our life might be with him or her always present, and we think of the implications of making a formal decree of our amorous intentions and desires. In our mind, we know what we are feeling, and we hope it will be reciprocated. Once we stop agonizing over it and say it aloud, it becomes real. We are suddenly excited, vulnerable—even exposed. There is a certain amount of relief, and there is a tangible understanding that we have now heard with our own ears.

2. **It creates reality**:
    We declare to ourselves that we indeed love the object of our affection. Emotions, feelings, and sentiments rising and falling in our conscious and unconscious mind materialize into reality. There is a sort of transference of power that takes place in the moment we speak it. Very literally, we take something nebulous (i.e. our thoughts) and shape them into a solid declaration. In that instant, the relationship between ourselves and the recipient is changed—the collective reality is changed. The words are out there, and they cannot be undone.

A similar shift or transference is also part of The Practice: Again, we create with our words. Realistically, much of what we say is purely utilitarian. Examples of this include everyday conversation in the workplace or at home: "She needs another cup of coffee," "I am thinking we should have pot roast for dinner," and "The game starts at 7 o'clock tonight" are just a few examples of innocuous, functional discourse. When we perform ceremonies or are in a state of prayer or meditation, we should be mindful of the spiritual and occult power of language. When we are in that luminous place—the zone or enraptured in our practice, words take on a hyper-potency that is not there otherwise. We operate under the authority of divinity, magic, and authentic power, and we speak across time and space and on several planes simultaneously.

THE CHERUB OF EZEKIEL

Hidden Uses of the Psalms

The Biblical Psalms have long been used as more than a simple book of poems or lyrics. Beyond the religious and historical significance of these songs, each syllable contains powerful invocations. When spoken aloud, we are calling on God by a specialized name reserved for specific purposes. The recitation of various passages incites Shekinah and dispatches various hosts of Heaven to act on behalf of the supplicant. Dormant covenants are activated when practitioners invoke the magico-religious power lying just below the surface of the Psalms.

While the content of the selections included here may not seem relevant to the situation cited, it is the speech patterns (phonemes, morphemes, etc.) that, when combined, bring about the desired result. These are included in the King James Version to retain some level of integrity to the original English translation. Some may argue this is only effective when one speaks the words in Hebrew, Aramaic, Latin, or Greek. To this I offer the following challenge: **See for yourself.**

EXORCIST RISING

The Original Exorcism Prayer

*Ancient Cabbalists and Jewish mystics intoned this psalm to drive demons out of the possessed. It is **the** original prayer of exorcism, and should be used with an extra measure of reverence based on its millennia of usage against Satan and his legions.*[33]

Psalm 91

He that dwelleth in the secret place of the most High shall abide under the shadow of the Almighty.

I will say of the LORD, He is my refuge and my fortress: my God; in him will I trust. Surely he shall deliver thee from the snare of the fowler, and from the noisome pestilence. He shall cover thee with his feathers, and under his wings shalt thou trust: his truth shall be thy shield and buckler.

Thou shalt not be afraid for the terror by night; nor for the arrow that flieth by day; Nor for the pestilence that walketh in darkness; nor for the destruction that wasteth at noonday. A thousand shall fall at thy side, and ten thousand at thy right hand; but it shall not come nigh thee. Only with thine eyes shalt thou behold and see the reward of the wicked.

Because thou hast made the LORD, which is my refuge, even the most High, thy habitation; There shall no evil befall thee, neither shall any plague come nigh thy dwelling.

For he shall give his angels charge over thee, to keep

---

[33] Trachtenberg, J. (1939). *Jewish magic and superstition: a study in folk religion.* (pp. 158-159) New York: Behrman's Jewish Book House.

thee in all thy ways. They shall bear thee up in their hands, lest thou dash thy foot against a stone.

Thou shalt tread upon the lion and adder: the young lion and the dragon shalt thou trample under feet. Because he hath set his love upon me, therefore will I deliver him: I will set him on high, because he hath known my name.

He shall call upon me, and I will answer him: I will be with him in trouble; I will deliver him, and honour him.

With long life will I satisfy him, and shew him my salvation.

EXORCIST RISING

De Profundis[34]

The 130th Psalm is used in Catholic Masses for the Dead (called a "Requiem Mass") and is also used to invoke God's protection from potential demonic or other types of spiritual attacks. This is a prayer that can be used to strengthen the exorcist and the afflicted. Because of its repetition throughout the ages, it is particularly potent—its efficacy is second only to Psalm 91.

Psalm 130

Out of the depths have I cried unto thee, O LORD.

Lord, hear my voice: let thine ears be attentive to the voice of my supplications. If thou, LORD, shouldest mark iniquities, O Lord, who shall stand? But there is forgiveness with thee, that thou mayest be feared.

I wait for the LORD, my soul doth wait, and in his word do I hope.

My soul waiteth for the Lord more than they that watch for the morning: I say, more than they that watch for the morning.

Let Israel hope in the LORD: for with the LORD there is mercy, and with him is plenteous redemption. And he shall redeem Israel from all his iniquities.

---

[34] De Profundis is the formal name assigned to this psalm by the Catholic Church. The Latin title translates to "from the depths."

NOAH TYSICK

Hidden Evils

The following two psalms reveal hidden enemies that are persecuting the oppressed without a rational cause (i.e. under demonic influence). Both are also effective in drawing an entity forward that may be hiding within the possessed. Once manifested, the demons can be cast out.

Psalm 7

O LORD my God, in thee do I put my trust: save me from all them that persecute me, and deliver me: Lest he tear my soul like a lion, rending it in pieces, while there is none to deliver.

O LORD my God, If I have done this; if there be iniquity in my hands; If I have rewarded evil unto him that was at peace with me; (yea, I have delivered him that without cause is mine enemy:) Let the enemy persecute my soul, and take it; yea, let him tread down my life upon the earth, and lay mine honour in the dust. Selah.

Arise, O LORD, in thine anger, lift up thyself because of the rage of mine enemies: and awake for me to the judgment that thou hast commanded. So shall the congregation of the people compass thee about: for their sakes therefore return thou on high.

The LORD shall judge the people: judge me, O LORD, according to my righteousness, and according to mine integrity that is in me. Oh let the wickedness of the wicked come to an end; but establish the just: for the righteous God trieth the hearts and reins. My defence is of God, which saveth the upright in heart. God judgeth the righteous, and God is angry with the wicked every day. If he turn not, he will whet his sword; he hath bent his bow, and made it ready.
He hath also prepared for him the instruments of death;

he ordaineth his arrows against the persecutors. Behold, he travaileth with iniquity, and hath conceived mischief, and brought forth falsehood. He made a pit, and digged it, and is fallen into the ditch which he made. His mischief shall return upon his own head, and his violent dealing shall come down upon his own pate.

I will praise the LORD according to his righteousness: and will sing praise to the name of the LORD most high.

Psalm 43

Judge me, O God, and plead my cause against an ungodly nation: O deliver me from the deceitful and unjust man. For thou art the God of my strength: why dost thou cast me off? why go I mourning because of the oppression of the enemy?

O send out thy light and thy truth: let them lead me; let them bring me unto thy holy hill, and to thy tabernacles.

Then will I go unto the altar of God, unto God my exceeding joy: yea, upon the harp will I praise thee, O God my God.

Why art thou cast down, O my soul? and why art thou disquieted within me? hope in God: for I shall yet praise him, who is the health of my countenance, and my God.

Emergency Protection

The 10th Psalm is known as the "24-hour shield of protection." Speaking the words of this prayer invokes divine protection in urgent situations. It is used for immediate relief from attacks for the exorcist and/or exorcistee. Nine consecutive recitations are recommended.

Psalm 13

How long wilt thou forget me, O LORD? for ever? how long wilt thou hide thy face from me?

How long shall I take counsel in my soul, having sorrow in my heart daily? how long shall mine enemy be exalted over me?

Consider and hear me, O LORD my God: lighten mine eyes, lest I sleep the sleep of death;

Lest mine enemy say, I have prevailed against him; and those that trouble me rejoice when I am moved.

But I have trusted in thy mercy; my heart shall rejoice in thy salvation.

I will sing unto the LORD, because he hath dealt bountifully with me.

Depression, Anxiety, and Mental Torment

Either of the following can be used to provide relief to those afflicted to the extent that it compromises their mental well-being. When medical and situational factors are not the cause, this psalm can be used to invoke the healing power of Shekinah.

Psalm 15

Lord, who shall abide in thy tabernacle? who shall dwell in thy holy hill?

He that walketh uprightly, and worketh righteousness, and speaketh the truth in his heart.

He that backbiteth not with his tongue, nor doeth evil to his neighbour, nor taketh up a reproach against his neighbour.

In whose eyes a vile person is contemned; but he honoureth them that fear the LORD. He that sweareth to his own hurt, and changeth not.

He that putteth not out his money to usury, nor taketh reward against the innocent. He that doeth these things shall never be moved.

Psalm 20

The LORD hear thee in the day of trouble; the name of the God of Jacob defend thee; Send thee help from the sanctuary, and strengthen thee out of Zion; Remember all thy offerings, and accept thy burnt sacrifice; Selah.

Grant thee according to thine own heart, and fulfil all thy counsel. We will rejoice in thy salvation, and in the name of our God we will set up our banners: the

NOAH TYSICK

LORD fulfil all thy petitions.

Now know I that the LORD saveth his anointed; he will hear him from his holy heaven with the saving strength of his right hand.

Some trust in chariots, and some in horses: but we will remember the name of the LORD our God.

They are brought down and fallen: but we are risen, and stand upright.

Save, LORD: let the king hear us when we call.

To Prevent Demonic Infestation

The following is a preventative psalm of protection. It can be used for a home, business, or other location. Practitioners may also use this as an invocation to protect people from demonic attacks and intrusions. Psalm 59 is a full spectrum assault against low spirits of all types and temperaments.

Psalm 59

Deliver me from mine enemies, O my God: defend me from them that rise up against me.

Deliver me from the workers of iniquity, and save me from bloody men.

For, lo, they lie in wait for my soul: the mighty are gathered against me; not for my transgression, nor for my sin, O LORD. They run and prepare themselves without my fault: awake to help me, and behold. Thou therefore, O LORD God of hosts, the God of Israel, awake to visit all the heathen: be not merciful to any wicked transgressors. Selah.

They return at evening: they make a noise like a dog, and go round about the city. Behold, they belch out with their mouth: swords are in their lips: for who, say they, doth hear?

But thou, O LORD, shalt laugh at them; thou shalt have all the heathen in derision. Because of his strength will I wait upon thee: for God is my defense. The God of my mercy shall prevent me: God shall let me see my desire upon mine enemies.

Slay them not, lest my people forget: scatter them by thy power; and bring them down, O Lord our shield. For the sin of their mouth and the words of their lips

let them even be taken in their pride: and for cursing
and lying which they speak.

Consume them in wrath, consume them, that they may
not be: and let them know that God ruleth in Jacob
unto the ends of the earth. Selah.

And at evening let them return; and let them make a
noise like a dog, and go round about the city. Let them
wander up and down for meat, and grudge if they be
not satisfied.

But I will sing of thy power; yea, I will sing aloud of thy
mercy in the morning: for thou hast been my defense
and refuge in the day of my trouble.

Unto thee, O my strength, will I sing: for God is my
defense, and the God of my mercy.

EXORCIST RISING

Protection from Demoniacs

Regardless of the degree of attachment or possession, you can invoke the 101st psalm to keep 'carriers' of the demonic out of your life. While some may not knowingly intend to bring grief upon you or your household, they carry an aura of negativity that is almost contagious. Recitation will repel the demoniac and minimize your exposure to their dark energy.

Psalm 101

I will sing of mercy and judgment: unto thee, O LORD, will I sing.

I will behave myself wisely in a perfect way. O when wilt thou come unto me? I will walk within my house with a perfect heart.

I will set no wicked thing before mine eyes: I hate the work of them that turn aside; it shall not cleave to me.

A froward heart shall depart from me: I will not know a wicked person. Whoso privily slandereth his neighbour, him will I cut off: him that hath an high look and a proud heart will not I suffer.

Mine eyes shall be upon the faithful of the land, that they may dwell with me: he that walketh in a perfect way, he shall serve me.

He that worketh deceit shall not dwell within my house: he that telleth lies shall not tarry in my sight.

I will early destroy all the wicked of the land; that I may cut off all wicked doers from the city of the LORD.

NOAH TYSICK

House Cleansing

Either of the following prayers are used to purge demonic or other low spirits from a home. This can include infestations that are active, latent, or suspected. Families may wish to join the exorcist in the recitation as a way of reclaiming their home.

Psalm 144

Blessed be the LORD my strength which teacheth my hands to war, and my fingers to fight: My goodness, and my fortress; my high tower, and my deliverer; my shield, and he in whom I trust; who subdueth my people under me.

LORD, what is man, that thou takest knowledge of him! or the son of man, that thou makest account of him!

Man is like to vanity: his days are as a shadow that passeth away.

Bow thy heavens, O LORD, and come down: touch the mountains, and they shall smoke. Cast forth lightning, and scatter them: shoot out thine arrows, and destroy them. Send thine hand from above; rid me, and deliver me out of great waters, from the hand of strange children; Whose mouth speaketh vanity, and their right hand is a right hand of falsehood.

I will sing a new song unto thee, O God: upon a psaltery and an instrument of ten strings will I sing praises unto thee.

It is he that giveth salvation unto kings: who delivereth David his servant from the hurtful sword.

Rid me, and deliver me from the hand of strange

children, whose mouth speaketh vanity, and their right hand is a right hand of falsehood: That our sons may be as plants grown up in their youth; that our daughters may be as corner stones, polished after the similitude of a palace: That our garners may be full, affording all manner of store: that our sheep may bring forth thousands and ten thousands in our streets: That our oxen may be strong to labour; that there be no breaking in, nor going out; that there be no complaining in our streets.

Happy is that people, that is in such a case: yea, happy is that people, whose God is the LORD.

Psalm 145

I will extol thee, my God, O king; and I will bless thy name for ever and ever. Every day will I bless thee; and I will praise thy name for ever and ever.

Great is the LORD, and greatly to be praised; and his greatness is unsearchable. One generation shall praise thy works to another, and shall declare thy mighty acts.

I will speak of the glorious honour of thy majesty, and of thy wondrous works. And men shall speak of the might of thy terrible acts: and I will declare thy greatness. They shall abundantly utter the memory of thy great goodness, and shall sing of thy righteousness.

The LORD is gracious, and full of compassion; slow to anger, and of great mercy.

The LORD is good to all: and his tender mercies are over all his works.

NOAH TYSICK

All thy works shall praise thee, O LORD; and thy saints shall bless thee. They shall speak of the glory of thy kingdom, and talk of thy power; To make known to the sons of men his mighty acts, and the glorious majesty of his kingdom. Thy kingdom is an everlasting kingdom, and thy dominion endureth throughout all generations.

The LORD upholdeth all that fall, and raiseth up all those that be bowed down. The eyes of all wait upon thee; and thou givest them their meat in due season. Thou openest thine hand, and satisfiest the desire of every living thing.

The LORD is righteous in all his ways, and holy in all his works.

The LORD is nigh unto all them that call upon him, to all that call upon him in truth. He will fulfil the desire of them that fear him: he also will hear their cry, and will save them.

The LORD preserveth all them that love him: but all the wicked will he destroy. My mouth shall speak the praise of the LORD: and let all flesh bless his holy name for ever and ever.

Addiction & Self-Destructive Behavior

When medical and psychiatric treatments fail, sometimes the problem may be spiritual in nature. Psalm 69 is an intercessory prayer for those suffering with addiction, disregard for their well-being, and other obvious forms of self-destruction and mutilation. The exorcist is pleading the cause of the afflicted and binding/banishing demonic influences out of their lives.

Psalm 69

Save me, O God; for the waters are come in unto my soul.

I sink in deep mire, where there is no standing: I am come into deep waters, where the floods overflow me. I am weary of my crying: my throat is dried: mine eyes fail while I wait for my God.

They that hate me without a cause are more than the hairs of mine head: they that would destroy me, being mine enemies wrongfully, are mighty: then I restored that which I took not away. O God, thou knowest my foolishness; and my sins are not hid from thee. Let not them that wait on thee, O Lord GOD of hosts, be ashamed for my sake: let not those that seek thee be confounded for my sake, O God of Israel.

Because for thy sake I have borne reproach; shame hath covered my face. I am become a stranger unto my brethren, and an alien unto my mother's children. For the zeal of thine house hath eaten me up; and the reproaches of them that reproached thee are fallen upon me.

When I wept, and chastened my soul with fasting, that was to my reproach. I made sackcloth also my garment; and I became a proverb to them. They that sit in the gate speak against me; and I was the song of the drunkards.

But as for me, my prayer is unto thee, O LORD, in an acceptable time: O God, in the multitude of thy mercy hear me, in the truth of thy salvation. Deliver me out of the mire, and let me not sink: let me be delivered from them that hate me, and out of the deep waters.

Let not the waterflood overflow me, neither let the deep swallow me up, and let not the pit shut her mouth upon me.

Hear me, O LORD; for thy lovingkindness is good: turn unto me according to the multitude of thy tender mercies. And hide not thy face from thy servant; for I am in trouble: hear me speedily. Draw nigh unto my soul, and redeem it: deliver me because of mine enemies.

Thou hast known my reproach, and my shame, and my dishonour: mine adversaries are all before thee. Reproach hath broken my heart; and I am full of heaviness: and I looked for some to take pity, but there was none; and for comforters, but I found none. They gave me also gall for my meat; and in my thirst they gave me vinegar to drink.

Let their table become a snare before them: and that which should have been for their welfare, let it become a trap. Let their eyes be darkened, that they see not; and make their loins continually to shake. Pour out thine indignation upon them, and let thy wrathful anger take hold of them. Let their habitation be desolate; and let none dwell in their tents. For they persecute him whom thou hast smitten; and they talk to the grief of those whom thou hast wounded.

Add iniquity unto their iniquity: and let them not come into thy righteousness. Let them be blotted out of the book of the living, and not be written with the righteous.

But I am poor and sorrowful: let thy salvation, O God, set me up on high. I will praise the name of God with a song, and will magnify him with thanksgiving. This also shall please the LORD better than an ox or bullock that hath horns and hoofs. The humble shall see this, and be glad: and your heart shall live that seek God.

For the LORD heareth the poor, and despiseth not his prisoners.

Let the heaven and earth praise him, the seas, and everything that moveth therein.

For God will save Zion, and will build the cities of Judah: that they may dwell there, and have it in possession.

The seed also of his servants shall inherit it: and they that love his name shall dwell therein.

NOAH TYSICK

Exorcism of a Violent Entity

Hostility and the threat of violence are very common behaviors in cases of severe possession. It's also not uncommon to observe defiance, arrogance, blasphemous and vile language, inappropriate laughing and smirking, and other bizarre or (potentially) intimidating conduct from one under demonic influence. This prayer is one that will subjugate even the most erratic of low spirits by virtue of praise expressed in the language. Within the atmosphere of these words, Shekinah will manifest.

Psalm 118

O give thanks unto the LORD; for he is good: because his mercy endureth for ever.

Let Israel now say, that his mercy endureth for ever.

Let the house of Aaron now say, that his mercy endureth for ever.

Let them now that fear the LORD say, that his mercy endureth for ever.

I called upon the LORD in distress: the LORD answered me, and set me in a large place. The LORD is on my side; I will not fear: what can man do unto me? The LORD taketh my part with them that help me: therefore shall I see my desire upon them that hate me.

It is better to trust in the LORD than to put confidence in man. It is better to trust in the LORD than to put confidence in princes.

All nations compassed me about: but in the name of the LORD will I destroy them. They compassed me about; yea, they compassed me about: but in the name of the LORD I will destroy them. They compassed me about like bees: they are quenched as the fire of thorns:

for in the name of the LORD I will destroy them.

Thou hast thrust sore at me that I might fall: but the LORD helped me. The LORD is my strength and song, and is become my salvation. The voice of rejoicing and salvation is in the tabernacles of the righteous: the right hand of the LORD doeth valiantly. The right hand of the LORD is exalted: the right hand of the LORD doeth valiantly. I shall not die, but live, and declare the works of the LORD.

The LORD hath chastened me sore: but he hath not given me over unto death. Open to me the gates of righteousness: I will go into them, and I will praise the LORD: This gate of the LORD, into which the righteous shall enter. I will praise thee: for thou hast heard me, and art become my salvation.

The stone which the builders refused is become the head stone of the corner. This is the LORD's doing; it is marvelous in our eyes. This is the day which the LORD hath made; we will rejoice and be glad in it.

Save now, I beseech thee, O LORD: O LORD, I beseech thee, send now prosperity.

Blessed be he that cometh in the name of the LORD: we have blessed you out of the house of the LORD.

God is the LORD, which hath shewed us light: bind the sacrifice with cords, even unto the horns of the altar. Thou art my God, and I will praise thee: thou art my God, I will exalt thee.

O give thanks unto the LORD; for he is good: for his mercy endureth for ever.

NOAH TYSICK

Divine Confusion

Shekinah brings perfect peace and order. Confusion, division, and chaos are manifestations of the dark. Spirit can invert the devices of demons back onto themselves. Rather than destroying and tormenting the victim, the legions become victims of each other. The power of uttering Psalm 48 cannot be understated.

Psalm 48

Great is the LORD, and greatly to be praised in the city of our God, in the mountain of his holiness. Beautiful for situation, the joy of the whole earth, is mount Zion, on the sides of the north, the city of the great King. God is known in her palaces for a refuge.

For, lo, the kings were assembled, they passed by together. They saw it, and so they marvelled; they were troubled, and hasted away. Fear took hold upon them there, and pain, as of a woman in travail.

Thou breakest the ships of Tarshish with an east wind. As we have heard, so have we seen in the city of the LORD of hosts, in the city of our God: God will establish it for ever. Selah.

We have thought of thy lovingkindness, O God, in the midst of thy temple. According to thy name, O God, so is thy praise unto the ends of the earth: thy right hand is full of righteousness.

Let mount Zion rejoice, let the daughters of Judah be glad, because of thy judgments.

Walk about Zion, and go round about her: tell the towers thereof.

Mark ye well her bulwarks, consider her palaces; that ye

may tell it to the generation following.

For this God is our God for ever and ever: he will be our guide even unto death.

Bibliography

Baxter, R. (1691). *The Certainty of the World of the Spirits.* Available from http://ebooks.library.cornell.edu/cgi/t/text/text-idx?c=witch;idno=wit012

Bazzett, M. (2012). Holy Mary, pray for us. *Catholic Culture.* Retrieved from http://www.catholicculture.org/culture/library/view.cfm?recnum=984

Buckland, R. (2002). *Practical candleburning rituals: Spells & rituals for every purpose.* Woodbury, MN: Llewellyn Publications.

Calamari, B. & DiPasqua, S. (1999). *Novena: The power of prayer.* New York: Penguin Putman, Inc.

Callan, C.J. & McHugh, J.A. (1925). *Blessed be God: A complete Catholic prayer book.* New York: P.J. Kenedy & Sons.

Ellis, J.T. & O'Boyle, P.A. (Eds.). (1953). *Mercy choir manual: The little office of the Blessed Virgin Mary and collection of prayers used by the religious sisters of mercy of the union in the United States of America.* New York: Frederick Pustet Company, Inc.

Gergen, M. M. & Gergen, K. J. (2003). Qualitative inquiry: Tensions and transformations. In N. K. Denzin & Y. S. Lincoln (Eds.). *The Landscape of qualitative research: Theories and issues.* (p. 579). Thousand Oaks: Sage Publications.

Harding, E.U. (1998). *Kali: The black goddess of Dakeshineswar.* Lake Worth, FL: Ibis Press/Nicolas Hays Books.

Harper, D. (2011-2012). Demon. *Online etymology dictionary.* Retrieved from http://www.etymonline.com/index.php?term=demon

Kirsch, J.P. (1911). St. Philomena. In <u>The Catholic Encyclopedia.</u> New York: Robert Appleton Company. Available from http://www.newadvent.org/cathen/12025b.htm

Kraut, R. (2010). Aristotle's Ethics. *Stanford encyclopedia of philosophy online.* Retrieved from http://plato.stanford.edu /entries/aristotle-ethics/

Marlbrough, R.T. (1998). *The magical power of the saints: Evocation and candle rituals.* Woodbury, MN: Llewellyn Publications.

Mezirow, J. (2000). *Learning as transformation: Critical perspectives on a theory in progress.* (pp. 9-11 & 17-18) San Francisco: Jossey Bass.

Owens, R.A. (2001). The Azusa Street Revival: The Pentecostal Movement begins in America. In V. Synan (Ed.) *The Century of the Holy Spirit: 100 years of Pentecostal and Charismatic renewal.* (p. 53) Nashville, TN: Thomas Nelson, Inc.

Pagels, E. (2003). *Beyond belief: The secret gospel of Thomas.* New York: Vintage Books.

Saint Gregory the Great. (n.d.). *The Life of St. Benedict.* Available from http://olrl.org/sacramental/benedictmedal.shtml

Simon. (2007). *Papal magic: Occult practices within the Catholic Church.* New York: Harper.

Smith, M.P. (1992). *Spirit world: Pattern in the expressive folk culture of African-American New Orleans.* Gretna, LA: Pelican Publishing Company, Inc.

SSA. (2011). Popular baby names: Top names of the 1960s. *United States Social Security Administration Website.* Retrieved from http://www.ssa.gov/OACT/baby names/decades/names1960s.html

Trachtenberg, J. (1939). *Jewish magic and superstition: a study in folk religion.* (pp. 158-159) New York: Behrman's Jewish Book House.

www.ingramcontent.com/pod-product-compliance
Lightning Source LLC
Chambersburg PA
CBHW061439040426
42450CB00007B/1125